The Brooklyn Dodgers

An Illustrated Tribute

The Brooklyn Dodgers

An Illustrated Tribute

by DONALD HONIG

ST. MARTIN'S PRESS

New York

For information, write : St. Martin's Press,
175 Fifth Avenue, New York, N. Y. 10010
Manufactured in the United States of America

Library of Congress Cataloging in Publication Data
Honig, Donald.
The Brooklyn Dodgers.
1. Brooklyn.   Baseball club (National League)—
History.
I.   Title.
GV875.B7H64   796.357′64′0974723   80-29309
ISBN 0-312-10600-9

Design by Dennis J. Grastorf

10   9   8   7   6   5   4   3   2

FOR ASSISTANCE IN PHOTO RESEARCH, the author
would like to express his appreciation and grat-
itude to The National Baseball Museum and
Library, and in particular to the knowledgeable
and helpful Jack Redding. Also, The Card
Memorabilia Associates, Ltd., of Amawalk,
New York, with a special thanks to Michael P.
Aronstein. One more word of thanks must be
said to those Brooklyn Dodger ball players who
so generously allowed the author to use photo-
graphs from their personal albums.

For My Daughter Catherine

Contents

The Brooklyn Dodgers

An Illustrated Tribute

Chapter 1

Beginnings

Frﾐﾐﾐ ﾐﾐﾐ ﾐﾐﾐﾐﾐﾐﾐﾐﾐ of the century onward it seemed to be the destiny of the Brooklyn Dodgers to have men of vision in positions of top management. Many of the game's cherished traditions were sent crumbling by the rampaging, innovative Larry MacPhail. Branch Rickey challenged and finally broke for all time the color line. And it was Walter O'Malley who broke baseball's geographical barrier by taking Brooklyn's beloved team clear across the continent.

But first there was Charles Ebbets. Born in New York in 1859, Ebbets was a shrewd, intelligent, hardworking man of diversified talents and interests. He was by turn a draftsman, a small-time publisher of novels and textbooks, and even served as an assemblyman in the State Legislature. It was baseball, however, that finally fired the imagination of the ambitious young man.

Baseball had been played in Brooklyn as far back as 1849, by clubs called Atlantic, Excelsior, Putnam, Eckford. These were amateur clubs but were among the best in the country, the Atlantics winning national championships in 1864 and 1866. Professional baseball did not come to Brooklyn until 1884 when a team was franchised for a league called the American Association which had been organized to rival the National League, then in business since 1876.

The new team was called the Dodgers, the name being adapted from "Trolley Dodgers," a nickname given to the citizens of the then-city of Brooklyn whose streets were being filled with a public transportation system consisting of clanging trolley cars.

In 1890 Brooklyn joined the National League. By that time Ebbets had been working for the club for six years. Charlie had made himself invaluable. He was active in every phase of the club's operation, selling tickets before the game, scorecards during the game, helping to clean up after the game, in addition to doing everything in the team office from emptying wastebaskets to making entries in ledgers. The curly-haired young man was eager, tireless, ambitious, and highly likable.

Whenever he could raise the cash, Ebbets bought stock in the team. In 1897 he was elected president of the club, though at that point his holdings amounted to around 10 percent. He was, however, the knowledgeable baseball man in the organization.

He was also devious. At that time, in the late 1890s, there was only one major league, the twelve-team National League. One of the dominant teams was the Baltimore Orioles, whose owner was a Baltimore brewer named Harry Von der Horst. In spite of his team's success, Von der Horst found himself taking a licking at the gate. Impressed with Ebbets and the operation in Brooklyn, he decided to invest some money there. In a maneuver that would be impossible today, Von der Horst ended up with controlling interest in both the Baltimore and Brooklyn clubs.

In order to protect his new investment, Von der Horst, to the delight of Brooklyn fans, began transferring some of his star players to the Brooklyn club. These included Wee Willie Keeler, Hughie Jennings, Joe Kelley, Iron Man McGinnity, and Jimmy Sheckard. To make these fellows feel at home, the Baltimore manager, Ned Hanlon, was also brought to Brooklyn. These machinations were sharply criticized in the newspapers, but in the absence of strong league control, nothing was done about it.

Hanlon led his combination of Brooklyn Dodgers and Baltimore Oriole expatriates to two first-place finishes in 1899 and 1900. There was, of course, no such thing as a World Series at that time, since no rival league existed. This situation was about to change, abruptly, bitterly, and permanently.

In 1901 the American League was formed and took to the field. In order to stock its eight teams, the new league was raiding the rosters of the National League, which had not encouraged its formation, to say the least. The Dodgers were among the heavy losers, seeing pitchers McGinnity and Wild Bill Donovan and outfielders Keeler and Kelley jump to the new league.

Realizing that these cutthroat practices would ultimately be ruinous for everyone, the two major leagues, using the common sense for which they would never become famous, declared a sullen truce in 1903. The National League magnanimously agreed to confer equal status upon its rival, the American League graciously promised to stop pirating players from what sportswriters have ever since reveled in calling "the senior circuit," and everyone settled down to the beatific sounds of well-smacked baseballs and spinning turnstiles. They even allowed their champions to meet in a postseason match—the World Series.

Meanwhile, Charles Ebbets kept solidifying his ownership of the Dodgers. Using borrowed money, he bought up Von der Horst's stock and by 1904 owned virtually all of the stock in the team.

An owner of a ball club is no different from the owner of anything else. Upon taking full control of the team, Charlie reelected himself president, raised his salary from $4,000 a year to $10,000, and further demonstrated what fun it was to be boss by trimming the pay of his manager, Ned Hanlon, down four grand to $7,500.

In 1905 the unhappy Hanlon guided the team to a resounding last-place finish, fifty-six and a half games behind John McGraw's Giants, and then resigned.

The new skipper was Patsy Donovan, brother of Wild Bill, a forty-year-old player just bringing his career to a close. Patsy improved things a little, bringing the club home fifth in 1906.

But there was really not much to cheer about for the fans who came out to Washington Park, the wooden firetrap which at that time was home for the Dodgers. Outside of first baseman Tim Jordan and outfielder Harry Lumley, there were few players of star quality wearing Brooklyn uniforms. The Dodger lineup in the latter years of the first decade was definitely not one to cause sleepless nights for opposing pitchers, who as a matter of fact should have had to pay to get into the ball park. The 1908 edition collectively batted a noiseless .213, which remains a league record for offensive futility. A symbol of Brooklyn's modest attack in these years was catcher Bill Bergen, the team's primary receiver from 1904 through 1911. In 1905 he reached his peak with a .190 average. One must assume that Bill either knew where the bodies were buried or else he was the greatest defensive catcher who ever lived.

Some fairly good pitchers had to watch their best efforts go to naught. These included Doc Scanlan, Harry McIntire, and a left-hander who was to become Brooklyn's first great star, Nap Rucker.

George Napoleon Rucker joined the Dodgers in 1907. The twenty-two-year-old native of Crabapple, Georgia, was an instant success, winning fifteen and losing thirteen for the fifth-place Dodgers.

Unfortunately for the gifted Rucker, one of the finest pitchers of his era, his career with the Dodgers coincided with one of the team's most dismal periods. During his first eight seasons the club never broke into the first division, nor did they ever play as well as .500 ball. Nevertheless, laboring valiantly and uncomplainingly, Rucker was able to post win totals of eighteen in 1908, seventeen in 1910, twenty-two in 1911, eighteen in 1912. With a few good sticks in the lineup Nap would have been virtually unbeatable. His lifetime ERA is 2.42.

Not only was the present discouraging, but the future seemed bleak. What was even more

galling for Ebbets was the success being enjoyed by McGraw's New York Giants. Outdrawing the Dodgers by sometimes as much as two to one, McGraw had forged his club into a tough, swaggering, highly efficient baseball-playing machine, with the remarkable Christy Mathewson at the crest.

McGraw loved provoking opposing players and fans, and nowhere did he enjoy lavishing his contempt more than he did in Brooklyn. Baseball's most antagonistic—and profitable—rivalry began in the first decade of the century, with McGraw's Giants consistently humiliating Ebbets' Dodgers.

One day in Brooklyn, while berating an umpire, McGraw heard Ebbets yell something from a box seat. The pugnacious Giant manager walked toward Ebbets and called something out. The livid Ebbets got to his feet and shouted, "Did you call me a bastard?"

"No," McGraw said. "I called you a *miserable* bastard."

Ebbets brought the incident before National League President Harry Pulliam, charging McGraw with rowdyism. But there was nothing Pulliam could do about it. Complaints were coming in all the time about McGraw, from opposing teams, umpires, fans. To no avail. John J. McGraw was a power unto himself.

As much as Ebbets disliked McGraw, there was no denying that when the Giants were in town Washington Park was packed. A lot of fans with live dollars in their pockets had to be turned away at the gate. Some enterprising residents in the tenements across the street accommodated numbers of disappointed fans by selling them spaces on rooftops and fire escapes at ten cents a head.

Those people on the rooftops and fire escapes did not escape Ebbets' canny eye. It was becoming more and more apparent to the Brooklyn team president that Washington Park would soon be obsolete. Sooner or later, he knew, Dodger fortunes would turn, and the team would field a winner. The idea of a winning team and inadequate seating in his ball park became an increasingly vivid nightmare for Ebbets, and somewhere around 1909 he began dreaming of a large, modern baseball facility and looking for a place to build it.

For the time being, however, Ebbets did not have to worry about a winning team squeezing his park's capacities. After a seventh-place finish in 1908, Patsy Donovan threw in the sponge. Next, Ebbets tried Harry Lumley as manager. Harry was a popular and well-liked player. His career, however, was just then being all but curtailed by a shoulder injury. Manager Lumley's first problem was replacing outfielder Lumley. No less than thirteen different men played in the Brooklyn outfield that year. One of them was a quiet, gentlemanly rookie from Missouri who got into only twenty-six games and batted .304. His name was Zachariah Davis Wheat, called Buck by his teammates and Zack by the fans, of whom he was to have many, perhaps more than any Dodger in history.

Wheat, who was part Cherokee, stood 5'10" and weighed around 170. Brought up on a farm, he was enormously strong, a left-handed hitter who sizzled line drives to all fields.

Zack was discovered playing for Mobile in the Southern Association by a man named Larry Sutton, a baseball buff with an uncanny eye for spotting talent, whom Ebbets had hired as a scout. On Sutton's recommendation, Ebbets bought Wheat from Mobile for $1,200.

Although he was to play into the era when the Dodgers began becoming populated with bright characters and outright eccentrics, Zack was never infected. He was soft-spoken, always the gentleman, and in eighteen seasons was never ejected from a game. Over a nineteen-year big league career (he played his last year for the Philadelphia Athletics in 1927), Zack hit for an average of .317.

Harry Lumley proved too easygoing as a manager and, after a sixth-place finish in 1909,

was demoted from player-manager to player, and Ebbets went manager hunting once more. His choice this time was Bill Dahlen, a forty-year-old veteran of nineteen big league seasons, five of them (1899–1903) spent playing shortstop for Brooklyn. Bill was considered a sound baseball man, aggressive and competitive. Ebbets congratulated himself on having made a good choice.

Dahlen could not improve upon 1909's sixth-place finish, despite a considerable advance in the team's won-lost record. But the winds of change were blowing stronger than Brooklyn fans perhaps realized. Both Tim Jordan and Harry Lumley played their last games in the big leagues that year before retiring because of injuries, Tim at the age of thirty-one, Harry only twenty-nine. Replacing Jordan at first base was another of the peripatetic Larry Sutton's finds, Jake Daubert. Sutton saw the twenty-five-year-old Pennsylvanian playing for Memphis and passed the word to Ebbets: "Buy him." The slick-fielding, sharp-hitting Daubert came to the Dodgers' Jacksonville, Florida, spring camp in 1910 and quickly made everyone forget about Jordan.

They called him "Gentleman Jake." When asked to explain the nickname, one of Daubert's teammates said, years later, "Why, because he was a gentleman." Daubert was well-dressed, courteous, intelligent. Jake's civilized qualities, however, were secondary to the fact that he could hit and field.

Also joining the Dodgers that season was a young catcher named Otto Miller, who was to remain in a Brooklyn uniform for thirteen years.

Wheat in left field and Daubert at first base gave the Dodgers' lineup a bit of sock, but they couldn't do it alone. Overall, the club batted .229. The pitching still pretty much began and ended with Rucker.

A closer look at the Brooklyn situation a few years later, however, showed more than a few sharp glints of light shining through. In 1913

Daubert's .350 batting average made him Brooklyn's first batting champion. Wheat had become a bona fide .300 hitter. They had a solid second baseman in George Cutshaw. A twenty-two-year-old rookie outfielder named Casey Stengel batted .272 and delighted the fans with his antics and the newspapermen with his wisecracks.

And that year there was, of course, a brand-new ball park.

Charles Ebbets in the 1890s.

Wee Willie Keeler around the turn of the century.

Wee Willie Keeler demonstrating the art of bunting. Keeler played for Brooklyn from 1899–1902. His four-year average was .353.

Joe (Iron Man) McGinnity, who earned his nickname by pitching doubleheaders. McGinnity pitched for Brooklyn in 1900, won twenty-eight games, and then jumped to the American League. A year later he returned to the National League, joining the Giants, where he became one of McGraw's greatest pitchers.

Jimmy Sheckard, who played for Brooklyn around the turn of the century, before being traded to the Cubs. Jimmy, an outfielder, hit .354 in 1901 and .332 in 1903, the year he led the National League with nine home runs and sixty-seven stolen bases.

Ned Hanlon.

Patsy Donovan, shown here while playing for Pittsburgh in 1894, had a seventeen-year career as an outfielder before taking over as Brooklyn manager in 1906.

7

Wild Bill Donovan, shown here in a Detroit uniform, pitched for Brooklyn from 1899–1902. Bill's best year was 1901 when he was 27–14. He later managed the Yankees.

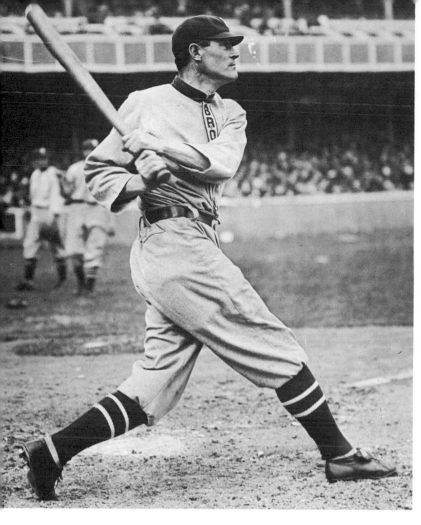

Tim Jordan, Brooklyn first baseman from 1906–09. He twice led the league in home runs, with thirteen in 1906 and twelve in 1908. A knee injury ended his career in 1910 at the age of thirty-one.

Harry Lumley had a fine rookie year in 1904, leading the league with nine home runs and eighteen triples. Harry, an outfielder, played for Brooklyn from 1904–10, when a shoulder injury ended his playing days. He managed the team in 1909.

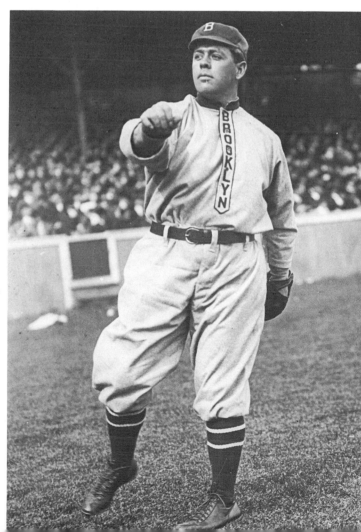

Bill Bergen caught for Brooklyn from 1904–11.
Perhaps the weakest hitter of all time, his
lifetime average for 947 games was .170. In
112 games in 1909 he hit .139.

Washington Park, home of the Dodgers until
Ebbets Field was built in 1913. This
photograph was taken on July 6, 1907, as
an overflow crowd watched Brooklyn shut
out the Cubs 7–0.

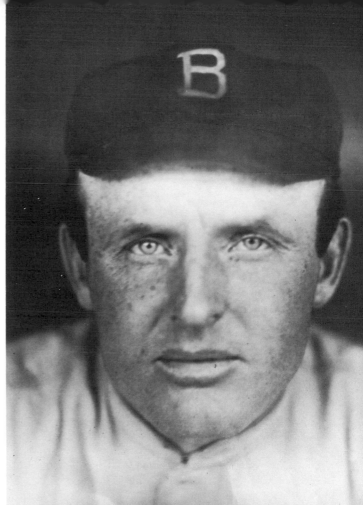

Right-hander Doc Scanlan pitched for
Brooklyn from 1904–11. His best year was
1906 when he was 19–14 with six shutouts.

Nap Rucker, perhaps the greatest of all Brooklyn left-handers.

John J. McGraw, in person.

Zack Wheat.

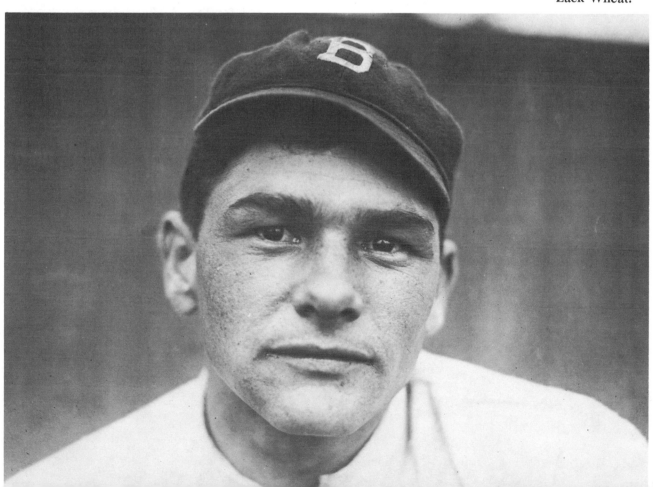

Jake Daubert.

Bill Dahlen, Brooklyn manager from 1910–13.

Bill Dahlen hitting ground balls to his infield in pregame workout at the Polo Grounds. Managers did that in those years.

Nap Rucker in 1911.

Casey Stengel in 1913.

This distinguished group of well-upholstered gentlemen are the Brooklyn Dodgers. The time: 1910. The place: Jacksonville, Florida. The occasion: spring training. Third from the left in the top row, wearing the derby, is Gentleman Jake Daubert. In the middle of the front row, wearing the straw hat, is Zack Wheat. Both were rookies that year.

Chapter 2

Uncle Robbie and the New Era

ALTHOUGH HIS BALL CLUBS gave him little reason to feel so, Charles Ebbets had great faith in baseball. In the winter of 1909 he made a speech at the club owners' winter meeting in New York. In the course of the speech he made an emphatic statement: "Baseball is in its infancy." Since the "infant" had at that time been around for some seventy years, the remark provoked a good deal of derisive comment in the newspapers. Ebbets' perception was, of course, more prophetic than even he could ever have dreamed.

That Charlie was not merely a phrasemaker was being borne out even then. The dream of a large, modern ball park had become an obsession with him. After months of driving and walking around Brooklyn, pondering the advantages and disadvantages of one parcel of land after another, he had finally found the place he was looking for.

It needed a prophet's eye to be able to imagine a huge, modern baseball plant rising upon the land as Ebbets originally saw it. What he finally settled on was a four-and-a-half-acre tract close to the northern reaches of Flatbush, a tract bordered by Bedford Avenue, Sullivan Street, Cedar Place, and Montgomery Street. It lay at the edge of a run-down neighborhood known as Pigtown. There was a scattering of shanties upon it, occupied by a more or less disreputable group of people. In the center of this unpromising chunk of Brooklyn real estate was a gaping hole into which the shanty people deposited their garbage and from which emanated the foulest vapors.

It took Ebbets nearly four years to achieve the purchase of the land he required, partially due to time spent looking for the rightful owners of this or that slice of ground, but also due to financial difficulties.

Dodger fans were becoming increasingly exasperated with their team, and consequently attendance was falling (it was less than 250,000 in 1912). Ebbets began beating a path to the doors of Brooklyn banks to obtain loans. The money was going out in two directions—to maintain a losing team and to keep buying the land for his dream park as it became available. Charlie was accumulating land and debts in equal measure. But he never for a moment wavered, sustained by those invincible twin faiths he had—in baseball and in himself.

By the end of 1911 Ebbets had finally acquired all the land he needed and filed deed to it. Early in March ground was broken. Ebbets himself, decked out in derby and elegant overcoat, took spade in hand and turned over the first scoopful of Flatbush earth. It took a suggestion more than persuasion for him to agree to call the place Ebbets Field.

He was still not out of the financial thickets, however. Even though work on the new park was moving ahead steadily, it was not assured of completion until Ebbets was forced to take in partners in return for a cash investment of $100,000. Charlie was not happy about this—pride of ownership was paramount with him—but he had little choice.

His partners, to whom Ebbets had to relinquish 50 percent of his stock, were the McKeever brothers, Ed and Steve, the latter known as "Judge" because of some early dabbling in politics. The McKeevers were highly successful builders and contractors with an enviable gift for making money. Although they were friends of long standing of Ebbets, their chief reason for sliding into the partnership was a hardheaded business one: they saw the rosy part of Charlie's dream and an opportunity to share in the profits.

When it finally opened for business, on April 9, 1913, Ebbets Field was more than just the triumphant realization of one man's dream—it was, in the context of its time, a magnificent structure, though still not the ball park that was to become so familiar to Brooklyn fans of a later

era. The left-field stands were to come in the 1920s, the double-deck stands in left and center in the 1930s. There were double-deck stands beginning at the right-field corner stretching around to the third-base area, at which point a concrete bleacher section began. The famous scoreboard in right field did not go up until the 1930s.

Originally the park, known in its later years as a "bandbox," was a pitcher's delight and a hitter's nightmare (the short right field being the exception). The left-field wall was nearly 420 feet from home plate and center field a titanic clout of 476 feet. (Right field was a cozy 301 feet.) When the park closed down in 1957, alterations and additions had brought left field to 343 feet down the line and the center field wall to a beckoning 393 feet.

Architecturally and financially the new ball park was a success. By trolley, horse and buggy, and by those newfangled automobiles, the fans came streaming to swing the turnstiles and pour through the magnificent tile-inlaid entrance rotunda to their seats. The basic problem, however, still remained unsolved. All that the fans had was a new and more splendid vantage point from which to watch their team lose. For lose the Dodgers did. Dahlen's 1913 team finished sixth—the eleventh consecutive season of second-division endings for the Brooklyns.

The few cheers that went up were for Daubert, Wheat, Cutshaw, and young Casey Stengel.

Stengel, who received his nickname from the initials of his birthplace, Kansas City, was another of Larry Sutton's finds. The color and humor of this vivid personality that New York fans were to relish on the field as late as 1965 were in evidence from the beginning. The dropout dental student from K.C. hit the big city as brash and unawed as a rookie could possibly be. Nor was he impressed by the opposition. One story has the rookie going into second base with his spikes high. The second baseman was the tough veteran Johnny Evers. When Evers warned the youngster about it, Stengel jumped to his feet and told Evers that this was the way he, Stengel, played ball and that Mr. Evers could be damned.

The problem now was pitching. Only two of Dahlen's pitchers won in double figures—Pat Ragan with fifteen and Nap Rucker with fourteen. To make matters worse, Rucker, only twenty-eight years old, was beginning to fade. The fine edge was gone from his fastball, and the snap on his marvelous curve was becoming a bit round.

In an effort to shore up his pitching, Ebbets obtained from the Cubs righthander Ed Reulbach, in his day one of the league's premier pitchers. The thirty-year-old veteran had enough left to run up a 7–6 won-lost record in his half season with the Dodgers. Ready to blossom into a winner, however, was hard-throwing righty Jeff Pfeffer, a bull of a man at 6'3" and 210 pounds.

Buoyed by some good hitters and still radiating in the success of his new ball park, Ebbets for the first time in years began feeling the itch of optimism. He also began feeling the need for a managerial change. He was fond of Dahlen, had no serious complaints about the way the club was handled, but Bill, through no fault of his own, had acquired the odor of losing, which was and is and always will be fatal for a manager. So, in the spirit of the new era he was trying to usher into Brooklyn baseball, Ebbets decided on a change.

Ebbets' first choice as Dahlen's replacement was Hugh Jennings, then in the middle of a fourteen-year reign as manager of the Detroit Tigers. But when Detroit refused ·to let Jennings out of his contract, Ebbets was forced to look elsewhere. Geographically, he did not look far. The man he chose was one of McGraw's coaches and former teammate during the glory days in Baltimore in the 1890s, Wilbert Robinson.

The man who was to become the beloved, good-natured, occasionally absentminded "Uncle Robbie" of lore and legend was fifty years old when hired by Ebbets. The good life had taken from him the trim figure he had cut as the Orioles' catcher—he now carried close to 230 pounds on his short, round frame—but not his kindly nature or his ability to laugh at the absurd, an ability which he would have to call upon many times during the eighteen seasons he presided over the Dodger dugout.

For a long time Wilbert Robinson's most memorable day on a ball field had occurred on June 10, 1892, when he connected for seven hits in a nine-inning game. He had awaiting him in Brooklyn, however, days and occasions much more memorable.

The archetypical Uncle Robbie story, and one of the best of all baseball stories, occurred during spring training at Daytona Beach in 1916. An attractive young aviatrix named Ruth Law was flying over the beach every day. A representative of a sporting goods firm talked her into taking him up one day so he could drop some golf balls onto the beach as a publicity stunt. One of the enthralled spectators who stood watching the golf balls dig into the sand was Wilbert Robinson. How it all got started is a little uncertain now, but Robbie, with an old catcher's pride, stated that he thought he could catch a baseball dropped from an airplane. It may have been said as an aside, but his players began egging him on until Robbie was stating unequivocally that he could catch a baseball dropped from an airplane.

Some of the players contacted Miss Law that evening and asked if she would participate in the scheme. She was delighted. Word got around, and a large crowd gathered on the beach the next day, in the middle of it a determined Wilbert Robinson with a catcher's mitt.

Miss Law would fly the plane, but someone was needed to drop the ball. None of the players was willing to take to the air—flying seemed only for the bold and the foolhardy in those days. Finally the trainer, Frank Kelly, volunteered.

Here the story once again becomes somewhat misty. Whose idea it was is lost to history (some say the practical joker was Stengel, a not improbable guess), but when Miss Law lifted her flying contraption into the air over the beach at Daytona that day she was carrying herself, Frank Kelly, and not a baseball but one large, round, juicy grapefruit.

The plane circled about, then swooped down to around four hundred feet, watched from the ground by the eagle eye of Wilbert Robinson, catcher's mitt at the ready. When he saw an object drop from the plane—Kelly proved a splendid bombardier—he began dancing about to position himself. Picking up speed as it plummeted, the grapefruit hurled directly toward Uncle Robbie who, if nothing else, was certainly proving his skill as a receiver. He was ready for it. Or at least he thought he was. The grapefruit came at him like a bomb, broke through his mitt, smashed against his chest, burst apart, and knocked Uncle Robbie flat on his keister. His startled words have been variously reported, but the ones most commonly agreed upon are, "Jesus! I'm killed! It's broke open my chest! Jesus! I'm covered with blood! Help!"

As he lay panting in the sand, Robbie had a mysterious experience—the taste of grapefruit was in his mouth. Indeed, he smelled all over like a grapefruit. When he realized what had happened—the grinning faces peering over him were the first tip-off—he got to his feet and strode away.

"If it was a baseball," he said later, "I woulda caught it. I had my hands on the goddamned thing, until it blew up."

The team showed improvement in Robbie's first year, 1914. Although finishing fifth, the club's .269 average led the league, with Daubert's .329 good enough for a second consecutive batting title. Wheat batted .319 and Stengel .314. Jeff Pfeffer came on like a forest fire, winning twenty-three.

Desperately in need of a shortstop, Ebbets went out and bought Joe Tinker from Cincinnati. Though thirty-three years old now, the front man in baseball's most famous and most overrated double-play combination still had some good baseball left in him and would certainly have shored up the infield. It was not to be, however.

In 1914 a new baseball war erupted, in the shape of a third major league, the Federal League. Repeating what the fledgling American League had done at the turn of the century, the Federal League began raiding the the National and American Leagues for players, enticing them with the lure of big bucks. One of the players who succumbed was Tinker, who joined the brand-new Indianapolis club. If this wasn't insult enough for Ebbets, injury soon followed when a Brooklyn Federal League team bankrolled by Robert Ward of Ward's Bakery set up shop in a refurbished Washington Park.

When the Brooklyn Feds made a lucrative offer to Daubert, Jake was prepared to accept it. Or so he told Ebbets, anyway. Charlie was frantic; he did not want to lose Daubert, particularly to his new in-town rivals. Jake, always a clear-sighted fellow, recognized opportunity when he saw it. He demanded, and received from a muttering Ebbets, a five-year contract at $9,000 per annum. Was that a lot of money in those days? The question was put to Burleigh Grimes years later. "I wouldn't say it was a lot," Burleigh replied; "I'd say it was *all* of it." He himself, Grimes lamented, was paid $1,800 a year when he joined Brooklyn in 1919.

Much to the relief of the National and American Leagues, the Federal League lasted but two seasons. The upstarts simply were not able to attract enough customers. Also, the established leagues made sure they kept their outstanding players by giving them salary increases—a technique sure to polish the loyalty of any employee.

In 1915 the team—now beginning to be called by newspapermen the "Robins" after their well-liked manager—finished third, their loftiest perch since 1902. Uncle Robbie had positioned his boys for a run at the pennant. In addition to putting Hy Myers into the outfield alongside Wheat and Stengel, the most significant moves were made to bolster the pitching staff. From the Philadelphia A's Ebbets picked up veteran righthander Jack Coombs, a thirty-game winner for Connie Mack just a few years before. Also joining the staff was a steady left-hander from Georgia named Sherrod Smith. Late in the season Ebbets picked up two more veteran pitchers, spitballer Larry Cheney from the Cubs and left-hander Rube Marquard from the Giants. Ebbets and Robbie felt they now had the team they wanted to go with in 1916.

Ebbets and his manager proved to be right about 1916, but not by much. It was a hard-fought pennant race and wickedly close. There were four contenders, all in the eastern division. The defending champs, the Phillies, led by Grover Cleveland Alexander's thirty-three victories, finished a scant two and a half games back. Behind them were the Braves, four games out, followed by the Giants, who trailed by seven.

Although the Dodgers hit well—their .261 average led the league—it was primarily through their patched-together, shrewdly handled pitching staff that they brought home Brooklyn's first pennant since the formation of the two-league structure. Pfeffer blazed the way with a 25–11 record, followed by Cheney, Smith, Marquard, and Coombs, all of whom won in double figures.

Daubert again led his teammates at bat with .316, with Wheat's .312 next. Robbie finally found the shortstop he needed in Ivy Olson, a hard-nosed player who would hold the position for the next half dozen years. Another newcomer, Jimmy Johnston, shared the outfield with Wheat, Stengel, and Myers. A valuable addition was the acquisition of McGraw's veteran catcher, John (Chief) Meyers. Meyers shared the catching with Otto Miller and was particularly adept at bringing out the best in his old Giant teammate Marquard.

The exciting pennant race, along with the sweet aroma of a brewing success, pushed attendance to a new high—almost 450,000.

Brooklyn's opposition in their first World Series was the Boston Red Sox. The Sox were a solid team though not a particularly formidable one (third baseman Larry Gardner, at .308, was their highest hitter), except on the mound. Their pitching was exceptionally strong. The staff included Carl Mays, Hubert (Dutch) Leonard, Ernie Shore, Rube Foster, and their ace, one of the great left-handers of the day, Babe Ruth.

Shore beat Marquard in the first game, 6–5, despite a four-run Dodger rally in the ninth which ended with the bases loaded and Daubert grounding out to short.

The second game remains one of the all-time classics in Series history, a game which sort of set a pattern for succeeding Brooklyn World Series adventures—something unusual, bizarre, unique, or exceptionally brilliant always seemed to happen when the Dodgers took to the field in October.

Left-handers Smith and Ruth squared off against each other other at Braves Field in Boston. (The Red Sox had decided to play their games not at their home field of Fenway Park but at Braves Field because of a larger seating capacity, which meant more money. The delectable lure of the dollar is not a thing unique to today's baseball.) With two out in the first inning, Hy Myers hit one past center fielder Tilly Walker and legged it around for an inside-the-park home run. In the Red Sox third,

Everett Scott tripled and came home on a grounder by pitcher Ruth, a good man to have batting ninth.

That was the scoring for the next ten innings as the two southpaws labored flawlessly into the fourteenth inning—an unprecedented and unequaled feat. In the bottom of the fourteenth inning the Red Sox won it on a walk, a sacrifice, and a pinch-hit single by a gentleman named Del Gainor.

The Dodgers rode the train back to New York that night, hoping to do better at Ebbets Field the next day. They did. The veteran Coombs beat the Red Sox 4–3, with relief help from Pfeffer. A two-run triple by Olson was the big blow.

It was downhill after that. Leonard beat Marquard 6–2 the next day, and the following day, back in Boston, Shore beat Pfeffer 4–1, and the first Brooklyn World Series was history. Part of that history was the last big league appearance of Nap Rucker. The great left-hander pitched two scoreless innings of relief in the fourth game, closing out his career at the age of thirty-two.

Preparing for the ceremonial opening of Ebbets Field, brass band and all. The date is April 5, 1913. The center-field bleachers would be built later. Note the size of the flag. Note, also, the freeloaders in the trees.

Mrs. Ed McKeever has just raised the flag,
surrounded by Brooklyn Dodgers in their
natty new team sweaters.

Ebbets Field, a year after it opened.

Charles Ebbets around the time of the opening of his new ball park.

Pitcher Ed Reulbach just before he was traded to the Dodgers in 1913. In his heyday with the Cubs he was almost unbeatable, posting a 61–15 record over one three-year period.

Wilbert Robinson. Note the club's nickname stitched on the sweater.

The Brooklyn and Boston teams are lined up
before a game at Ebbets Field, April 11, 1914.

Big Jeff Pfeffer became the ace when Rucker
faded. The hard-throwing right-hander won
twenty-three in 1914 and twenty-five in 1916.
He pitched for Brooklyn from 1913–1921.

Wee Willie Keeler returned to Brooklyn as a
coach for the Federal League club in 1914.

Jack Coombs getting ready for a game in the Dodger clubhouse, in 1916.

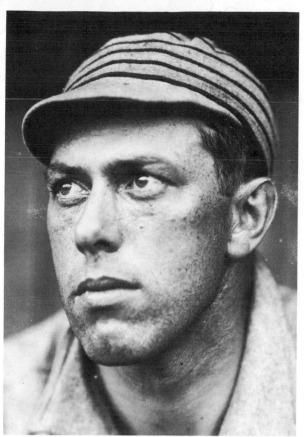

George Cutshaw, Brooklyn's fine second baseman from 1912–17. He batted .280 in his rookie year, his best mark as a Dodger.

Through the years the Dodgers would obtain many players who were past their prime. Jack Coombs, shown here with the Philadelphia Athletics for whom he won thirty games in 1910 and twenty-nine the next year, was one of them. In 1915 he joined the Dodgers and won fourteen games that season, twelve the next.

Obtained in 1915 from the Cubs, for whom he had won twenty-six games in 1912, Larry Cheney pitched for Brooklyn until 1919. His best year for the Dodgers was 1916 when he was 18–12.

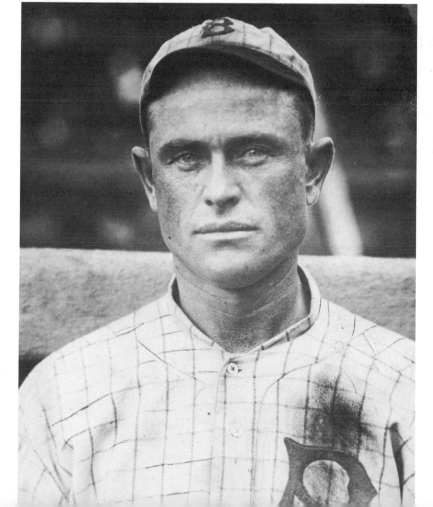

Left-hander Rube Marquard was another pitcher who joined the Dodgers with his great days behind him. After winning big for McGraw for three years, he was dealt to Brooklyn in 1915. His best years for Brooklyn were 1916–17, when he was 14–6 and 19–12. He pitched for the Dodgers until 1920.

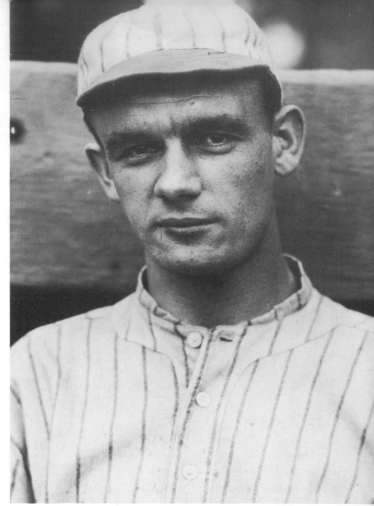

Sherrod Smith, who pitched for Brooklyn from 1915–22, turned in two brilliant World Series efforts. In 1916 he lost to Babe Ruth 2–1 in fourteen innings, and in 1920 he beat Cleveland in the third game, 2–1. He later lost game six by a 1–0 score. Smith's World Series ERA of 0.89 is one of the lowest in history. Never a big winner, his best year was 14–8 in 1915.

Hy Myers played the outfield for Brooklyn from 1909–22, hitting over .300 three times. His best year was 1922, when he hit .317. Myers led the league in triples in 1919 and 1920.

John Tortes (Chief) Meyers had been
McGraw's regular catcher for seven years
before being dealt to the Dodgers in 1916.
The Chief (a full-blooded Indian) batted .247
for Brooklyn in that pennant-winning year.
He was traded to the Braves the next season.

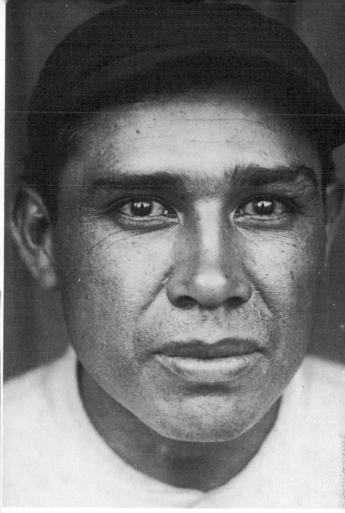

Ivy Olson was Brooklyn's regular shortstop on
the 1916 and 1920 pennant winners. He was
with the Dodgers from 1915–24. His best year
was 1919, when he batted .278 and led the
league in hits.

The opposing managers in a traditional pose
before the opening of the 1916 World Series.
Wilbert Robinson on the left, and Bill
Carrigan of the Red Sox.

Brooklyn's battery for their first World Series game ever, Rube Marquard, left, and Chief Meyers. The date was October 7, 1916, in Boston.

The Dodgers, who had stolen 187 bases during the regular season, could manage only one theft during the Series. It is the seventh inning of the third game, and Zack Wheat has just stolen second base. The second baseman is Hal Janvrin, being backed up by shortstop Everett Scott.

Chapter 3

A World War and Another Pennant

IN 1917 AMERICA WENT TO WAR, and Brooklyn came back to earth. The 1917 Dodgers made the 1916 club look like an accident. No other team in history had ever dropped from first place to seventh in the course of a single season, but this is exactly what Uncle Robbie's boys did. Attendance, which usually goes up the year after a pennant has been won, took a sharp nose dive, to 221,000, or less than half of the previous year.

Ebbets and Robbie decided changes were in order. After the 1917 season they shipped Cutshaw and Stengel to Pittsburgh in a deal for pitchers Al Mamaux and Burleigh Grimes. The trade was not popular with Dodger fans, Cutshaw and Stengel being two favorites. But Robbie, who prided himself upon being a shrewd judge of pitching talent, had scored a bull's-eye. Mamaux would pitch decent ball for a few years, but Grimes was destined to become one of Brooklyn's greatest pitchers.

"Boily," as he was fondly called by his adoring Brooklyn fans, was one tough-nut character. A rugged competitor, he could be buzzsaw mean on the mound, quick with a fastball under the chin of any hitter he thought was crowding him. And any hitter who didn't like it was welcome to come out and discuss it. Grimes, it was said, "was more than able to defend his point of view."

Grimes was one of the great spitball pitchers, when that pitch was still a legal weapon in a pitcher's arsenal. He would chew the fiber from the bark of a slippery elm and then load up the ball. "That ball would break like hell," he later said, "away from right-hand hitters and in on lefties."

Ebbets and Robbie were ready to make other moves, but by now the country was seriously into the war, and players were beginning to go off to serve their country. The pitching staff was particularly hard hit, with Pfeffer going

34

into the Navy and lefty Clarence Mitchell and righty Leon Cadore joining the Army.

Because of the war the season ended early in 1918, baseball closing down in the first week of September. It was fine with the Dodgers, nestling in fifth place. Wheat's league-leading .335 average was the year's only bright note.

Shortly before the opening of the 1919 season, Ebbets announced the trade of his longtime first baseman Jake Daubert to the Reds for outfielder Tommy Griffith. Jake had long been a pain in Ebbets' side—the side Charlie kept his wallet—and the owner had been waiting for the chance to deal away Gentleman Jake.

To replace Daubert, Ebbets picked up veteran Ed Konetchy from the Braves. Big Ed—anybody over six feet tall was called "Big" in those days—was near the end of the trail but had enough left to give the Dodgers a few good years.

Nineteen nineteen found the Dodgers finishing fifth. It was a dreary season. Unknown to all, however, the future was being rung in, for on January 31 in the town of Cairo, Georgia, a robust little fellow named Jack Roosevelt Robinson was born, and on March 17 in St. Louis an incomparable bundle of talent named Harold Patrick Reiser came into the world. Meanwhile, in Ekron, Kentucky, Harold Henry Reese was already a year old.

Help was on the way.

Though the birthrate for future stars dropped dramatically in 1920, the year was nevertheless a solid success, both artistically and financially. In winning their second pennant, the Dodgers set a new club attendance record with 808,000 —360,000 more than their previous high, set in the pennant-winning year of 1916.

For the Dodgers it was a year for oddball happenings. On May 1 in Boston they and the Braves played one of baseball's most memorable games—a twenty-six inning marathon that ended in a 1–1 tie. What etched the game forever in history was the fact that both starting pitchers went all the way, Leon Cadore for Brooklyn and Joe Oeschger for Boston. These two run-of-the-mill pitchers put on what remains the most heroic dual feat of pitching in baseball history. Before darkness mercifully put an end to it, Oeschger had given up but nine hits and four walks through the twenty-six innings, Cadore fifteen hits and five walks.

That night the Dodgers returned home to play a Sunday game with the Phillies. It was a one-game series, Sunday ball then being illegal in Pennsylvania. After that game, they were scheduled to return to Boston. They lost to the Phillies in thirteen innings, returned to Boston that night and lost to the Braves the next day in nineteen innings, 2–1. So their three-day slate showed fifty-eight innings of baseball—more than six games' worth—with the only thing achieved one of those charmingly bizarre footnotes to Brooklyn baseball history.

This haplessness, however, proved atypical this year. Through June, July, and August they played steady ball, hovering around first place and occasionally ducking into the top spot for a few days.

Grimes had one of his greatest years, winning twenty-three and losing eleven. It was Pfeffer's last full year in Brooklyn, and the big right-hander made it a good one, finishing at 16–9. Cadore, Mamaux, Smith, and Marquard also won in double figures. Wheat, getting better as he got older, batted .328, followed by Konetchy at .308 and Myers at .304. Robbie's new third baseman, Jimmy Johnston, who had been an outfielder on the 1916 club, batted .291. Newcomer Pete Kilduff was at second and Ivy Olson at short. Otto Miller did the bulk of the catching and batted .289, his best mark ever. Not a bad team.

In September they moved into first place, established a small lead and held onto it, improving it now and then. They clinched the pennant on September 27 and at the end were seven games ahead of second-place New York.

The American League champions were the Cleveland Indians, led by player-manager Tris Speaker, whose .388 batting average was a splendid piece of managing. The Indians were, in fact, stocked with .300 hitters; along with Speaker these included Larry Gardner, Elmer Smith, Charlie Jamieson, Steve O'Neill, and Joe Sewell. Cleveland's first baseman was Doc Johnston, older brother of the Dodgers' Jimmy.

In right-hander Jim Bagby the Indians boasted a baseball rarity, a thirty-game winner, though even some of his teammates intimated that Jim wasn't really that good. The true ace of the staff, they suggested, was spitballer Stanley Coveleski.

In those years baseball was experimenting with a five-out-of-nine World Series, in order to pile the green a little higher. (This blatant bit of pocket-squeezing was discontinued a few years later, and the Series returned to its present four-out-of-seven structure which, like 90 feet between bases, seems somehow just right.)

The Series went seven games, and the Dodgers scored exactly eight runs, being shut out three times. Coveleski, true to form, won three games. Brooklyn jumped out to a 2–1 lead in games, but the Cleveland pitching became too much for them after that as the Indians took the next four in a row, giving up just two runs in the process.

The Dodger heroes were Grimes, who shut the Indians out in the second game, and Sherry Smith, who three-hit them in the third game. Wheat hit .333 and Olson .320; most of the other averages needed a microscope to be seen.

The story of the 1920 World Series is to be found in game five, played in Cleveland on October 10 and won by the Indians by the rather dreary score of 8–1. But in this game there occurred two "firsts" and one spectacular "only."

The first "first" occurred, appropriately enough, in the first inning. With Grimes on the mound, leadoff man Charlie Jamieson singled. The next batter, Bill Wambsganss, also singled. Speaker beat out a bunt. Bases loaded. There had never been a jackpot homer in World Series play. Well, the doors of history swung wide as cleanup man Elmer Smith launched a shot over the right-field fence.

The next "first" occurred in the Cleveland fourth. With two men on base, pitcher Bagby homered into the center-field stands—the first pitcher ever to hit a home run in a World Series. Soon after, a baffled and fuming Burleigh Grimes left the game, wondering what Tris Speaker knew. Grimes's exasperation was founded on a remark Speaker made after the great spitballer had shut the Indians out in the second game. "Grimes," the Cleveland manager said, "won't win another game in the Series." The remark puzzled Grimes, since Speaker was not given to making such rash statements. Later that winter Burleigh found out what had given Tris such assurance.

"We had a fellow named Pete Kilduff playing second base," Grimes said. "He's out there, and he can see the catcher's signs. Before each pitch he's picking up some sand and putting it in his glove. If it's not a spitter, he drops the sand. If it's going to be a spitter, he keeps it in his glove. He's doing that, you see, so if the ball is hit to him, he'll get some of the wet off of it so it won't slip when he throws it. Christ, I don't know why the hell he had to do that—fellows were throwing it from short, from third. Anyway, it didn't take long for somebody to pick that up, and all the hitters had to do was watch Kilduff." What they did was lay off the spitter and set for the fastball. Never a retiring sort, Grimes later "discussed" it with Kilduff. "He never cared a hell of a lot for me after that," Burleigh muttered.

Down 7–0 in the top of the fifth inning, the Dodgers came to bat. They had been peppering Bagby fairly steadily, but a few double plays had kept them from scoring. Kilduff opened with a single. Otto Miller did likewise. The next batter was relief pitcher Clarence Mitchell, one of the western world's few left-handed spitballers and a good hitting pitcher. Robbie let him bat, for which baseball historians and folklore specialists must always be grateful. For an instant it looked like managerial genius, for Mitchell tied into one and sent a screamer out to center field. Or so it seemed. It certainly seemed so to Kilduff and Miller as they began excitedly to churn around the basepaths.

But there was a second baseman named Bill Wambsganss. Steady, efficient, he was born to play thirteen years in the major leagues and hit .259, one of those gray batting averages guaranteed to give a man the protection of obscurity. But at this moment Bill Wamby, as he was generally called and as he was squeezed into those wonders of economy known as box scores, was to kick obscurity in the duff and achieve the dream play of all dream plays. Years later Bill Wamby described it to Lawrence S. Ritter for Ritter's incomparable *The Glory of Their Times.*

"Jim Bagby was pitching for us, and he served up a fast ball that Mitchell smacked on a rising line toward center field, a little over to my right—that is, to my second-base side. I made an instinctive running leap for the ball and just barely managed to jump high enough to catch it in my glove hand. *One out.* The impetus of my run and leap carried me toward second base, and as I continued to second I saw Pete Kilduff still running toward third. He thought it was a sure hit, and was on his way. There I was with the ball in my glove, and him with his back to me, so I just kept right on going and touched second with my toe (*two out*) and looked to my left. Well, Otto Miller, from first base, was just standing there, with his mouth open, no more than a few feet away from me. I simply took a step or two over and touched him lightly on the right shoulder, and that was it. *Three out."*

Just like that. It was, and remains, the only unassisted triple play in World Series history.

After a moment of stunned silence, the fans got the message and began to cheer, and straw hats came flying out of the stands—that's what fans threw in those days.

One last footnote to that notable game. When he next came to bat in the eighth inning, Mitchell grounded into a mere double play—a slight improvement, but still not enough.

The next day a former Dodger, left-hander Walter Mails, beat Smith 1–0. Coveleski ended it a day later with a 3–0 shutout.

The disheartened Dodgers disbanded for the winter, hoping for better things in 1921. It was a pleasant hope, and a reasonable one. But the drought was now ready to set in, and it would be twenty-one years—most of them bumbling, some of them hilarious—before a Dodger team would take the field for a World Series. After all, Pee Wee Reese was still only two years old and Pete Reiser a mere year and a half. As precocious as they would later prove themselves to be, they still weren't ready.

Al Mamaux pitched for Brooklyn from 1918–23. His best year was 1920, when he was 12–8.

Tommy Griffith, whom the Dodgers obtained in exchange for Jake Daubert in 1919. Tommy stayed until 1925. He hit .312 in 1921 and .316 the next year.

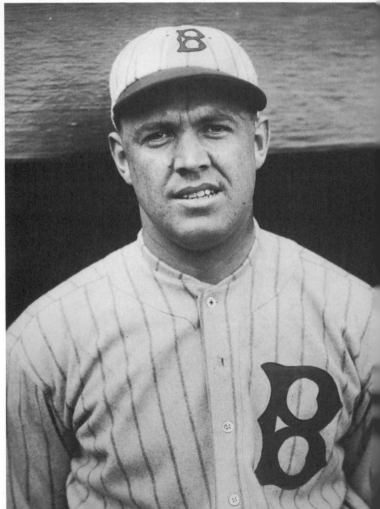

Burleigh Grimes.

Otto Miller in 1917.

Ed Konetchy. Big Ed had twelve big-league seasons behind him when the Dodgers obtained him from the Braves in 1919. He batted .308 for the 1920 pennant winners, then was traded to the Phillies the next year. He was another in the long line of good-hitting Brooklyn first basemen.

Pete Kilduff was with the Dodgers from 1919–21. He batted .272 as second baseman for the 1920 pennant winners.

Leon Cadore.

Joe Oeschger.

For one day, at least, they were the most durable pitchers in baseball history.

Stanley Coveleski pitched three complete game victories against the Dodgers in the 1920 Series.

The opposing managers obliging the photographers before the opening of the 1920 World Series. Uncle Robbie is on the left, Cleveland manager Tris Speaker on the right.

Another pair of glad-handers at the 1920 World Series. This time they're brothers, first baseman Doc Johnston of the Indians on the left, and third baseman Jimmy Johnston of the Dodgers on the right. Jimmy Johnston played for the Dodgers from 1916–25. From 1921–23 Jimmy batted .325, .319, .325.

41

Action at home plate in the 1920 Series.
Brooklyn's Tommy Griffith is out trying to
score in the third inning of the second game.
Steve O'Neill is the catcher, Tommy Connolly
the umpire.

Bill Wambsganss is about to tag a stunned Otto Miller and complete the only unassisted triple play in World Series history. Umpire Hank O'Day is about to make the call. Pete Kilduff has already rounded third base and is just now looking back over his shoulder. Cleveland third baseman Larry Gardner and Bill Dinneen are taking it all in. (*The Bettmann Archive, Inc.*)

Wambsganss poses with his victims the next day. From left to right: Bill Wamby, Pete Kilduff, Clarence Mitchell, Otto Miller. Appropriately, Bill is the only one smiling.

Chapter 4

The Daffy Dodgers

WHAT WAS TO BECOME the popular perception of the Dodgers—of clowns, buffoons, traffic jams on the basepaths, madcap fans rooting zealously for chronic losers—began to take shape in the 1920s. Uncle Robbie was at least partially responsible for the image. He seemed to watch it all with a certain sense of detachment as if he might have other, more serious business on his mind. He also seemed genuinely fond of his athletes, like a grandfather with too many rascally grandchildren bounding mischievously about, sighing at their boyish antics.

How did he handle his players? "I think they handled him more than he handled them," Burleigh Grimes said. "We had Ivy Olson. He wanted to make a hit in every ball game. Very laudable. But the problem was he never wanted to bunt. Uncle Robbie always sat in back of that concrete post we had in the dugout. When Olson was up and he knew a bunt was in order, he'd keep moving around in the batter's box to keep that post between him and Robbie so Rob-

bie couldn't flash him the sign. We'd watch Robbie move in one direction, Olson in the other. The bunt sign was a clenched fist, and here's Robbie sliding around on the bench with that fist clenched, and there's Olson up at the plate, ducking around to keep that post between them. Finally Robbie would say, 'Ah, the hell with it.'"

Then there was a blithe spirit named Chick Fewster who put in some time at second base for the Dodgers in the twenties. One day he made the double play backwards. Instead of crossing the bag and going to his right while he threw to first, he took the throw from the shortstop and spun all the way around, making a complete circle and then firing to first. When he came into the dugout at the end of the inning, a bemused Uncle Robbie said, "I've been in baseball for forty years, and I want to ask you a question: What the hell kind of a way is that to make a double play?"

"How'd you like it?" Fewster asked.

"I didn't," Robbie said.

The man considered by many as the greatest of all Brooklyn pitchers joined the Dodgers at their Jacksonville spring camp in 1922. At the age of thirty-one he was a rather mature rookie, having been in professional baseball since 1912, pitching here, there, and everywhere, always with enough stuff to get another job when he needed one. His name was Arthur Clarence (Dazzy) Vance, and he possessed the fastest fastball and the damnedest curveball of his time. He was big and strong, which Robbie liked, and he was witty and colorful, which the fans liked.

Dazzy had won twenty-one games for New Orleans in 1921, but even at that his acquisition was fortuitous. The Dodgers were looking for catching help—Otto Miller was slowing down—and New Orleans had the man they wanted, Hank DeBerry. DeBerry spoke so highly of Vance to Larry Sutton that the scout recommended Dazzy's purchase along with DeBerry's.

Vance had had trials with Pittsburgh and the Yankees in 1915 and again with the Yankees in 1918, posting a composite 0–4 record. The big guy was wild and suffered from a sore arm now and then. But when he reached Brooklyn in 1922, he was ready. Coming to the bigs at the age of thirty-one, he still won 197 games. He led the league in strikeouts his first seven seasons. His greatest season came in 1924 when he won twenty-eight, lost six, completed thirty of thirty-four starts, led in earned-run average and strikeouts, and was voted the league's Most Valuable Player.

That 1924 season was Brooklyn's lone bright spot in an otherwise sorry decade during which they were to finish in sixth place six times in seven seasons. But in 1924 they chased McGraw to the finish line, coming up one and a half games short.

Burleigh Grimes won twenty-two games, teaming with Vance to win fifty between them. Spittin' Bill Doak (he threw a moist one), a mid-season acquisition from the Cardinals, was

11–5. After that, however, the pitching wasn't much to speak of.

Jack (Jacques) Fournier, acquired from the Cardinals the year before, played first base and led the league with twenty-seven home runs. (Things were destined to get even better around the bag, for on April 4 of that year a strapping baby named Gilbert Raymond Hodges was born in Princeton, Indiana.) The ageless Zack Wheat, getting better as time went on, hit .375.

After that giddy season, however, the Dodgers took a lease on sixth place, finishing there for the next five seasons.

On April 18, 1925, just as the Dodgers and Giants were getting ready to begin a three-game series at Ebbets Field, Charles Ebbets died. The man who had seen so clearly into baseball's future, and whose faith in the game had never wavered, was sixty-six. The game went on as scheduled that day, the consensus being that Charlie would never have wanted a Dodger-Giant game postponed, no matter what the reason.

Ed McKeever took over as acting president, but not for very long. The day Ebbets was buried in Brooklyn's Greenwood Cemetery was a cold and blustery one. McKeever took to his bed the next day, complaining of a heaviness in the chest. Pneumonia quickly developed, and within a week he was dead.

Soon after, Wilbert Robinson was elected president of the club. During the time it took for him to acquaint himself with his new duties, Robbie temporarily left the dugout, appointing Wheat acting manager. After a few weeks, though, he began to itch to return to uniform. In a typical Uncle Robbie maneuver, he returned to the dugout and sat there in uniform while Wheat ran the club—or tried to, the presence of two managers creating a good deal of confusion all around. Finally Robbie took over again as manager, and Wheat, a bit perplexed and more than slightly disgruntled, returned to left field.

What the Dodgers were losing in efficiency

they were gaining in color, and it was in the spring of 1926 that the most colorful Dodger of them all reported to Brooklyn's Clearwater training camp. He was a tall, slim, light-haired, buck-toothed twenty-two-year-old slugger who was to become central to more incidents quaint and bizarre than any other Dodger, and would finally emerge as the embodiment of the total legend of Brooklyn baseball. His name was Floyd Caves Herman, but nobody ever called him anything but Babe.

Babe was a first baseman when he reported. He was a bit awkward around the bag, so Robbie—who took an immediate liking to the big kid—sent him to the outfield. Babe had his troubles out there for a while, but what baseball historians have tended to overlook is that Herman eventually became a fine outfielder, with a strong and accurate arm, and even a skillful base runner, all legends notwithstanding.

But there was one thing Babe Herman could do right from the beginning and do better than most men who ever played big league ball. He could hit. He hit for distance and he hit line drives that were murderous, all of it accomplished with the sweetest, most natural swing in baseball. (When Ted Williams first appeared on the scene, awed observers, groping for comparisons, likened the youngster's incomparable swing to Herman's.) From 1928 through 1930 his averages were .340, .381, .393. Hornsby called him the hardest hitter in the major leagues, McGraw described him as one of the greatest natural hitters he had ever seen, and Grover Cleveland Alexander said there was no way to pitch to him. But because history will choose the good story over plain statistics every time, Herman's reputation lies not in the record book but in folklore.

Herman's adventures started in his rookie year, on August 15, 1926, to be exact (just a month before the birth of a handsome tyke named Edwin Donald Snider in Los Angeles). The scene is Ebbets Field. The Dodgers are playing the Braves. It is the bottom of the seventh inning. The score is tied, 1–1. The Dodgers have three men on base (each, at this point, one feels obligated to say, on a different base). These men, about to gallop into history, are, on first, Chick Fewster; on second, Dazzy Vance; on third, Hank DeBerry. There is one out. The man at the plate is Babe Herman. Left-hander George Mogridge hangs a curve, Babe gives it a bash all the way to the top of the right-field fence, and the basepath merry-go-round begins. In an interview given many years later, Herman can still see it happening:

"The ball was hit so hard that it bounced back far enough for the second baseman, Doc Gautreau, to run out and retrieve it. He picks it up and fires it to the shortstop, Eddie Moore, who's covering second, just as I'm sliding in there. I'm safe. Now, I'm lying on the ground and I hear Gautreau yelling to Moore to throw the ball home. I look around and catch a glimpse of somebody stopped midway between third and home. I figure it's Fewster. Who else could it be? DeBerry had scored easily, and Vance had been on second, so I was sure he'd scored, too. It had to be Fewster.

"I figured Fewster was going to be caught in a rundown between third and home, and that while he was jockeying around I could make third. So as soon as Moore throws the ball home, I get up and light out for third, keeping an eye on that rundown. I go sliding into third, and by gosh who's jumping into the air to get out of the way of my spikes but Chick Fewster! He comes down behind me, and I look up to see the umpire, Charley Moran, scratching his head. Then he says, 'Hey, Babe, you're out for passing Fewster on the baseline.' That was a little technical, but he was right.

"At that moment, Vance comes running back to third, jumps on the bag with both feet, and says, 'Ha, ha, I'm safe.' 'Yeah, you big Airedale,' I said to him, 'and you're the only one who is.' So I got up and started walking away. Fewster says to me, 'Well, I guess I'm out, too.' So we both started walking away. Fewster goes over and picks up his glove and gets ready to play second base. Remember now, he's still not out. Gautreau, who'd retrieved the ball in right field, now comes running in and takes it from the third baseman. He tucks it into his glove and walks nonchalantly over to Fewster and says, 'Chick, look what I got.' Then he touches Fewster with the ball. When he does that, the umpire yells, 'Fewster, you're out!' Chick looks at him and says, 'I thought I was out five minutes ago.'"

The legend persists that Herman tripled into a triple play; what he actually did was double into a double play (because of some atrocious baserunning by Vance). But what he also did that day was knock home the winning run with his famous base hit. "Robbie knew that," Herman said. "That's why he never said anything about the mix-up at third base. We won the game."

In 1930 Herman put together the most devastating season in Dodger history. He set six team records that year that still stand: batting average (.393), slugging average (.678), total bases (416), extra base hits (94), runs scored (143), hits (241). But, typical of Herman's reputation, even more memorable than that Herculean season is something that never even happened.

The event that did not happen, happened in 1928, in Ebbets Field. Robbie took Herman out late in a game in which the Dodgers were far ahead. Into Babe's spot in right field—the sun field—was sent utility outfielder Al Tyson. The sun was at that moment setting, blazing into the right fielder's eyes from between the upper and lower grandstands. Somebody hit a line drive out to Tyson, the ball disappeared in the sun, and Tyson (a first-rate glove) lost it. The ball hit him on top of the head and skipped out to the wall.

No announcement of the change in right field had been made, and the writers, daydreaming through the long, dull game, never noticed it. What they did see was the right fielder get skulled by a ball, and because they believed it was their beloved Babe they made sure the story was highlighted. The story remains highlighted, despite Herman's good-natured denials and the testimony of eyewitnesses. In the face of time and tireless repetition, truth has been known to concede a point.

Coaching third for the Dodgers in Herman's rookie year of 1926 was one of Robbie's teammates on the old Baltimore Orioles, Joe Kelley, a great player in his day. One afternoon Herman hit a screamer over first base. The ball went down into the Brooklyn bullpen and rolled under the bench there. Babe rounded second base, only to see Kelley holding him up, so he put on the brakes and scrambled back to second. To his astonishment, the right fielder was just then coming up with the ball. On the next play Herman got to third base, and when he did he called Kelley over.

"Joe," he said, "what's coming off here? You stop me at second when the outfielder hasn't picked up the ball yet."

"Babe," Kelley whispered, putting his hand on Herman's shoulder, "I want to tell you something. Without my glasses, I can't even see who's pitching."

"So why don't you wear 'em?" the unappeased Herman demanded.

"Wear glasses on a ball field?" Kelley asked indignantly. "Never."

And so they dragged on through years of high-spirited futility. The cast kept changing—Wheat left after the '26 season, Grimes was traded to the Giants in '27—but sixth place continued to beckon and odd things continued to occur. Like the time Spittin' Bill Doak keeled over and almost drowned in a bucket of water. Well, not quite, but that's how the story went. It was a blistering hot day in Pittsburgh, and Bill was pitching against the Pirates. After each inning he came in and sat down on the bench and leaned over and lowered his hands into a bucket of ice water, his face turned florid from the unforgiving heat. Around the sixth inning the exhausted Doak leaned one time too many, and over he went, passing out and landing head-first in the bucket. "Hey!" Robbie yelled. "There goes old Bill! Save him!" They saved him. After a little slapping around, Spittin' Bill was revived and went out and won his ball game.

Finally, in 1930, powered by Herman's .393 average, they broke the sixth-place pattern and finished fourth. It was, however, a strong fourth-place finish, just six games out. They actually led the league for a good part of the summer before slipping back. The unexpected excitement shook the fans out of their lethargy, and a new club attendance record was set—1,100,000.

But now there was dissension in the front office. Robbie and Steve McKeever were barely on speaking terms. McKeever and some of the other club directors felt it was time for a change —Robbie had been there for eighteen years now. After the 1931 season the reign of Wilbert Robinson came to an end. Informed that his contract would not be renewed, the sixty-eight-year-old Robinson resigned. He retired to Dover Hall, a tract of land outside of Brunswick, Georgia. He involved himself in the management of the Atlanta ball club, then in the Southern Association. Early in August 1934, he tripped and fell down a flight of stairs. Suffering several fractures, he was rushed to the hospital. There, on August 8, he died, six months after the death of his old friend and bitter rival John McGraw.

The new manager was Max Carey, in his heyday with the Pirates the National League's premier base stealer. Carey was Robbie's antithesis in many ways. Where Robbie had been plump and soft and affable, Max was lean and fit and quite reserved, and something of a disciplinarian. His daring, flashy play for twenty years had earned him the respect of players and fans alike.

As one of his coaches, Carey hired Casey Stengel, bringing this popular character back to Brooklyn after a fifteen-year absence. The Dodgers took a chance and obtained former home-run king Hack Wilson, hoping this powerful tree stump of a man could regain his past glory. (He couldn't.) There was a new young pitcher, a high-kicking right-hander with blazing speed named Van Lingle Mungo. He was hailed as the new Dazzy Vance, the original model now forty-one years old and about to depart after the '32 season.

Babe Herman's average had dropped to .313 in 1931, and the club slashed his salary accordingly. The Babe wouldn't take it and stayed home in Glendale, California. Neither side would budge. Then, on March 14, Dodger fans were shocked to learn that their favorite had been traded to Cincinnati. Along with Herman went hard-hitting young catcher Ernie Lombardi, who had been second-string to Al Lopez. In return the Dodgers got a light-hitting backup catcher, Clyde Sukeforth, and two good infielders, Tony Cuccinello and Joe Stripp.

Carey brought them home third, outfielder Lefty O'Doul gave Brooklyn another batting champion with a .368 mark, young Mungo showed he was for real, but otherwise it was an unremarkable Dodger club.

Those were hard years, for the Dodgers and for the country at large. The full, deadening impact of the Great Depression was being felt everywhere, including at the Ebbets Field turnstiles. Those were years when the Dodgers were unable to crack the half-million mark at the gate. Perhaps a contending team might have helped, but they were as uninspired and uninspiring a set of teams as the Dodgers ever fielded, those clubs of the middle 1930s. The new steel-and-concrete bleachers so hopefully built in the early thirties were almost always empty.

In the summer of '33 there were rumors that Carey was on the way out. McKeever gave Max more than assurance about his job; he signed him to a contract for next season.

The 1934 season was to begin with an insult and end on a note of grim satisfaction. In between, however, it wasn't much fun. The insult occurred during the big leagues' spring meetings in New York. Bill Terry, manager of the world champion Giants, was being interviewed by a group of writers. He was asked where he thought his competition would come from. St. Louis? Chicago? Somebody asked him about the Dodgers. Terry, never one for wisecracks, got one off this time.

"Brooklyn?" he asked with a smile. "Is Brooklyn still in the league?"

Coming from the manager of the Giants, it stung, particularly since Brooklyn was indeed barely in the league, financially and artistically. The crack never bothered the players, but it did leave Dodger fans incensed, fans having a more emotional attachment to a ball club than most players. Terry's appearances at Ebbets Field that summer were received with a heckling so fervent and intense that even the aloof Terry was surprised.

Another surprised gentleman that year was Max Carey. His signed contract notwithstanding, Carey was suddenly fired in February and his coach Casey Stengel hired. Being fired in February produced from Max the deathless line: "What the hell were they expecting me to do, win the pennant over the winter?" So it was a year during which the Dodgers were paying two managers—one to manage and one not to.

Stengel, then as later, was popular with his players, the fans, and especially the press—no manager ever provided better copy. But a sixth-place club was a sixth-place club, and not even Stengel's wizardry could affect the natural order of things.

What happened on the last two days of the season, however, made an entire summer's agony worthwhile. The Giants and the Cardinals had been fighting it out all year and came down to the final weekend in a flat-footed tie. The Cardinals were finishing at home against the Reds; the Giants were at home for two with the Dodgers.

On Saturday, with the Polo Grounds packed with screaming, bloodthirsty Dodger fans, Mungo burned his fastball past the Giant batters for a 5–1 win. To make the day perfect for Brooklyn, the Cardinals won in St. Louis, 6–1.

The next day was even better. Overcoming an early 4–0 Giant lead, the Dodgers pounded the cream of Terry's staff—Fred Fitzsimmons, Hal Schumacher, and Carl Hubbell—and won in ten innings, 8–5. It proved to be academic when Dizzy Dean shut out the Reds, but nonetheless satisfying. By helping beat the Giants out of a pennant, the Dodgers had done the next best thing to winning it themselves, and their fans were able to go off into the grim Depression winter with a measure of satisfaction.

Recognizing that the problems of the club were not Stengel's fault, the board of directors signed him to a new contract through the 1937 season. There were handshakes all around and some bravely optimistic words for the upcoming season. But the financial picture was gloomy. The club was losing money steadily, and just as steadily the directors were marching over to the Brooklyn Trust Company and arranging new loans in order to keep the team afloat.

If there was little professionalism on the field, the same might be said for the front office. During the 1936 World Series between the Giants and the Yankees, the directors made an announcement: Casey Stengel was out as manager. For the second time in three years the Dodgers, struggling against bankruptcy, would be paying two managers.

The new man was another old favorite—Burleigh Grimes. After leaving Brooklyn in 1926 he had pitched for the Giants, Pirates, Braves, Cardinals, Cubs, and Yankees, then managed in the minor leagues for a few years. Now he was back, still the tough, no-nonsense man with the same hair-trigger temper that would keep him constantly embroiled with the umpires.

The team that he took over was not designed to soothe Burleigh's already grainy disposition. Outside of Buddy Hassett at first base, the veteran Heinie Manush in the outfield, and a round Babe Phelps behind the plate—they called him "Blimp"—there wasn't much to cheer about. Right-handers Luke Hamlin and Max Butcher topped the staff with eleven wins each. But the fire in Van Mungo's fastball was beginning to cool, and the rest of the pitchers were more helpful sitting on the bench than standing on the mound.

Grimes did make a few moves that were to pay off in the future. He obtained a young third baseman from the Pirates, Harry (Cookie) Lavagetto, who ten years later would deliver the single most famous base hit in Dodger history, and in a mid-season swap with the Giants added thirty-five-year-old knuckleballer Freddie Fitzsimmons. To some, Fitz looked to be over the hill, but that look was deceiving. A red-blooded New York Giant, Fitz described the trade to the Dodgers as "the blackest day of my life." But Fat Freddie would soon come to love Brooklyn, and the feeling would be mutual.

Burleigh was also the brains behind another deal that was completed after the end of the 1937 season. He sent Joe Stripp and three other players to the Cardinals for their thirty-two-year-old shortstop, a dazzling glove man whose average that year was an emaciated .203. Behind him was a good, solid playing career; ahead lay excitement and glory and controversy. His name was Leo Durocher.

Dutch Ruether, left, shown here with fellow left-hander Slim Sallee when both were with Cincinnati, was traded to Brooklyn after the 1920 Series. Dutch gave the Dodgers good service, winning twenty-one in 1922 and fifteen the next year. He pitched in Brooklyn for four years.

Burleigh Grimes lacing up his spikes during spring training at Hot Springs, Arkansas, February 1923.

Dazzy Vance.

Zack Wheat in 1924.

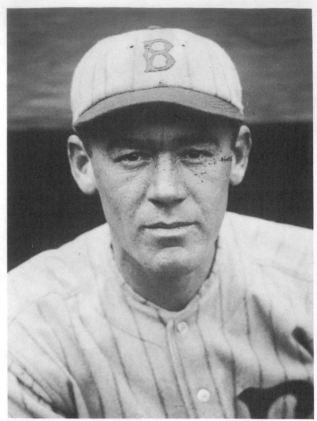

Hank DeBerry, Vance's favorite catcher. Hank was with Brooklyn from 1922–30 and had a lifetime average of .267.

It's May 19, 1925, a pleasant afternoon at Ebbets Field, and Dazzy Vance is receiving $1,000 in gold from baseball writer Fred Lieb for having been voted the National League's Most Valuable Player for the 1924 season. Just visible over Lieb's right shoulder is Judge Kenesaw Mountain Landis, who had been hired as baseball's first commissioner a few years before.

A leaky glove kept Jacques Fournier bouncing around the big leagues for many years. But there were never any holes in his bat. Joining the Dodgers in 1923, the powerful first base-man reeled off averages of .351, .334, .350; knocked in over a hundred runs each season; and led the league with twenty-seven home runs in 1924. Jacques' last year with Brooklyn was 1926.

Chick Fewster played only one season for the Dodgers, 1926, batting an unmemorable .243. Chick, however, sort of blundered into immortality when one afternoon at Ebbets Field he found himself at third base with teammate Vance coming at him from one direction and teammate Herman from another.

Babe Herman. For a while he was so good that they called him "Brooklyn's Babe" to differentiate him from that other Babe, also a right fielder, who played for the Yankees.

Joe Kelley—too proud to wear glasses on the field.

Jess Petty pitched for the Dodgers from 1925–28. The left-hander's most productive year was 1926 when he was 17–17. His 2.84 ERA was third best in the league that year.

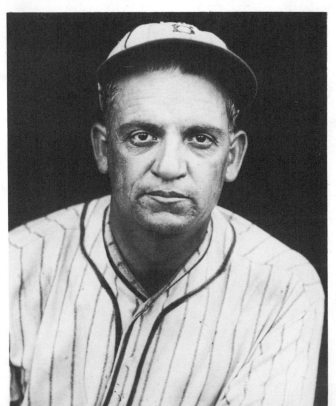

56

Shortstop Dave Bancroft was thirty-seven when he reached Brooklyn in 1928. Still, he gave the Brooks 149 games at the position and batted .247. In his younger days with the Giants he was one of the best.

Jesse Barnes, one of McGraw's aces earlier in the decade, finished up with the Dodgers in 1926–27.

Bill Doak, the man who almost drowned in a bucket of water. Spittin' Bill put in three seasons with Brooklyn after a long career with the Cardinals. He was 11–5 in 1924, retired for two years, then came back in 1927 and was 11–8.

Team president and manager Wilbert Robinson is pleased as he watches his ace, Dazzy Vance, signing a contract at the team's Clearwater, Florida, training camp on March 18, 1929. Vance had been holding out for $25,000. His smile indicates he got it.

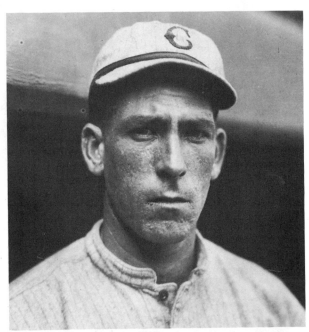

Curveballer Dolf Luque, shown here in his prime with Cincinnati, joined the Dodgers in 1930, when he was forty years old. Nevertheless Luque, the first great Cuban major leaguer, won fourteen and lost eight that year.

Del Bissonette joined the Dodgers in 1928 and replaced Fournier at first base. He had several fine years with the Dodgers, hitting .320 with twenty-five home runs in '28 and batting .336 in 1930. A leg injury suffered in 1932 cut short his career.

Left-hander Watson Clark pitched for the Dodgers from 1927–37, except for a brief period in 1933 when he was traded to the Giants, who traded him back to the Dodgers the next season. Clark's best year was 1932 when he had a 20–12 record.

Dazzy Vance pitching to Kiki Cuyler at Ebbets Field in the summer of 1930. The famous right-field scoreboard has not yet been built, nor have the center-field stands.

This Dodger battery bridges the generations. On the left is right-handed pitcher Jack Quinn who came to the big leagues in 1909 and who was almost forty-seven years old and still pitching when this picture was snapped, on April 14, 1931. Quinn was in thirty-nine games that year for the Dodgers, winning five, losing four, and saving fifteen. His catcher is a youthful Al Lopez, then a twenty-two-year-old just starting his second full season with the Dodgers. Al was Brooklyn's regular catcher through the 1935 season.

Johnny Frederick was one of Brooklyn's better ball players during his years with the team, 1929–34. In his first two years he batted .328 and .334, collecting 206 hits in each of those seasons and leading the league with 52 doubles his first year. In 1932 Frederick hit six pinch-hit home runs, still a record for one season.

Highpockets George Kelly was another who wound up a distinguished career playing with the Dodgers. Kelly played first for Brooklyn for part of the 1932 season, his last in the majors.

Max Carey—real name Maximilian Carnarius
—in 1932. Max finished his twenty-year
playing career in the Brooklyn outfield, playing for the Dodgers from 1927–29.

Still another veteran first baseman for the
Dodgers. Joe Judge, after eighteen years in
the American League, is shown here in 1933
reading his contract with Steve McKeever.
But Joe was not there long; an injury limited
him to forty-two games and a .214 average.

Glenn Wright, formerly a great shortstop with Pittsburgh, was with Brooklyn from 1929–33. Hampered by an arm injury through most of his Dodger days, Glenn did give the team one outstanding season in 1930, when he hit .321 and drove in 126 runs.

When Wright departed, Lonny Frey, shown here on the left shaking hands with Arky Vaughan of Pittsburgh, became the Brooklyn shortstop, a job he handled well until traded to the Cubs after the 1936 season. Frey's best year was 1934, when he hit .284.

In 1932 the Dodgers obtained Hack Wilson (shown here as a Giant rookie in 1924), hoping the onetime home-run leader could regain his former style. But the only thing the thirty-two-year-old Wilson led the league in was strikeouts, although he did hit twenty-three home runs and bat .297. The Dodgers had been hoping for more. Hack lasted until midway through the 1934 season, leaving the big leagues shortly thereafter.

Ernie Lombardi caught one year for the Dodgers, 1931. He hit .297. Unable to dislodge Al Lopez from the number-one catching job, he was traded to Cincinnati, where he became one of the hardest-hitting catchers in history.

Clyde Sukeforth, shown here in spring training in 1934, was backup catcher for the Dodgers from 1932–34. Sukeforth later became a trusted scout for Branch Rickey and was the man Rickey asked in 1945 to bring Jackie Robinson to meet him.

One of the finest hitters who ever lived, Frank (Lefty) O'Doul joined the Dodgers in 1931 in a deal with the Phillies. Lefty hit .336, followed it with a league-leading .368 in 1932, then slipped a bit next year and was traded to the Giants along with Watson Clark for first baseman Sam Leslie.

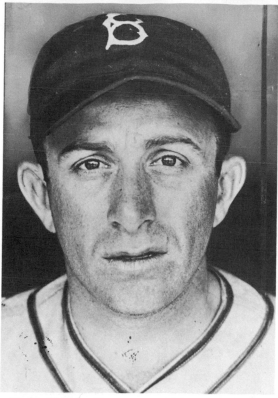

Tony Cuccinello was Brooklyn's second baseman from 1932–35. His best year was 1935, when he hit .292.

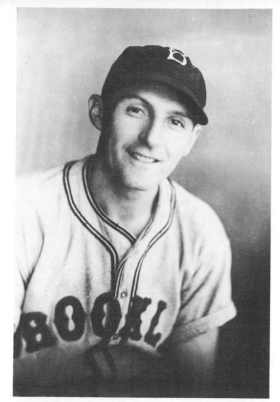

Jersey Joe Stripp was at third base for the Dodgers from 1932–37. He hit .300 four times for Brooklyn, with a high of .317 in 1936.

Sam Leslie played first base for the Dodgers in 1934–35, batted .332 and .308, and was then dealt back to the Giants.

Emil (Dutch) Leonard pitched for Brooklyn from 1933–36. He was 14–11 in 1934, then tailed off and was sent to the minors. He later resurfaced as a knuckleball pitcher for Washington and went on to pitch for another sixteen years in the big leagues.

Len Koenecke joined the Dodgers in 1934. The twenty-eight-year-old outfielder did well, batting .320. He was, however, a difficult character, constantly breaking club rules. In September of the following season Stengel finally ran out of patience with Len and ordered him to leave the club. Koenecke flew to Chicago, but became drunk on the way and caused such a disturbance he was put off the plane when it landed in Detroit. He then hired a small private plane and asked to be flown to Buffalo. On the way to Buffalo, obviously drunk, he tried to take over the plane's controls. In a midair scuffle with the pilot and copilot he was struck on the head with a fire extinguisher. When the plane came down in Toronto, the nearest airport, Koenecke was dead.

Dodger manager Casey Stengel and Judge Landis in 1935.

Brooklyn was the last stop in Waite Hoyt's twenty-one-year career. The once-great Yankee pitcher was 8–9 in 1937, started off poorly the next year, and was released.

Do you see anything scandalous about Stanley "Frenchy" Bordagaray's face? Well, in 1936 the management of the Dodgers did. They were scandalized when Frenchy showed up in spring training with his upper lip thusly decorated, and he was sternly ordered to shave or else. Frenchy shaved, went on to bat .315, and was traded to the Cardinals the next year. He returned to Brooklyn in 1942 and helped bring some respectability to the club during the war years.

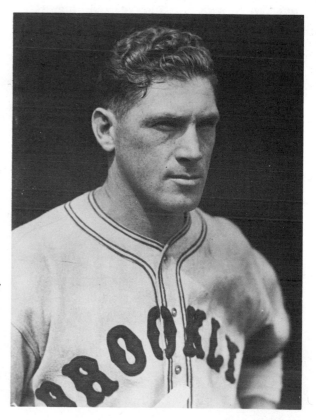

John "Buddy" Hassett gave Brooklyn another .300-hitting first baseman in 1936–37 before moving to the outfield to make way for Camilli in 1938, after which season he was traded. A singles hitter, Buddy batted .310, .304, and .293 for Brooklyn.

It's 1937, and new skipper Burleigh Grimes doesn't have much more than Van Lingle Mungo's right arm going for him. It didn't go too far. Mungo, only twenty-six, was fading quickly. He was 9–11 that year and thereafter ceased to be a factor for the Dodgers.

An American League hitting star for fourteen years, Heinie Manush was thirty-six when he landed in Brooklyn in 1937. Heinie set a fine example with a .333 average. But it was a last, heroic gasp. He was gone the next year, heading for Cooperstown.

Chapter 5

Hurricane Larry

THE FORTUNES OF THE Brooklyn Dodgers were at this point at their lowest ebb. Ford Frick, at that time president of the National League, was becoming increasingly concerned about the franchise, once one of the league's strongest. Deciding to take a hand, Frick went to the board and urged them to hire a new general manager, someone not only with a track record but a person with flair and initiative.

"Like whom?" he was asked.

"Larry MacPhail," Frick said.

Larry MacPhail was not a breath of fresh air. He was a hurricane. He was a man in motion, aggressive, dynamic, brimming with ideas. A showman. Forty-eight years old when he took over in Brooklyn in January 1938, MacPhail had been a college athlete, a lawyer, a successful businessman, a captain in the First World War (his most famous caper was an attempt to kidnap the German Kaiser after the war, an at-

tempt that came ridiculously close to succeeding). Brought into baseball by Branch Rickey in 1930 to run the Columbus club of the American Association, Larry was a huge success and soon went on—as was his wont—to better things.

A few years later he was running the Cincinnati club for Powel Crosley. Taking a moribund, near-bankrupt franchise, MacPhail began putting together the team that would eventually win pennants in 1939–40. In 1935 he introduced night baseball to the major leagues. He also began broadcasting Cincinnati's home games. The man he hired for the job was a smooth, articulate, honey-voiced Southerner named Walter (Red) Barber. The years in Cincinnati were like a trial run for what MacPhail was to do in Brooklyn.

MacPhail's arrival virtually coincided—it was almost symbolic—with the death of Steve McKeever, the last of the old guard. McKeever's stock passed to his daughter, Mrs. James Mulvey. But that hardly mattered. MacPhail was running the club, and everybody was giving him plenty of room. More importantly, the Brooklyn Trust Company was lending him whatever he needed. In spite of the team's mounting debt to the bank, the president, George V. McLaughlin, believed in MacPhail and was willing to go along with him.

MacPhail spent several hundred thousand dollars refurbishing Ebbets Field, repairing and painting the stands, replacing broken seats, cleaning up the rest rooms and clubhouses. He also announced that henceforth Dodger games would be broadcast, by Red Barber, who was only too happy to join Larry in Brooklyn. The decision to broadcast broke what had been a gentleman's agreement between the three New York clubs not to "give away their games for nothing" over the airwaves. The Giants and Yankees were upset by the decision, but there was nothing they could do about it.

What interested the fans most, however, was what Larry was going to do to improve the club. Less than two months after taking over, Mac-Phail gave them an inkling—he bought first baseman Dolph Camilli from the Phillies for $50,000. A flashy fielder with a potent bat, Camilli gave the Dodgers the power hitter they sorely needed. Camilli was MacPhail's primary player acquisition that first year, because there were limits on the amount of cash the bank would advance, and much of it—something like $100,000—was going into the light towers that Larry was building on the roof of Ebbets Field. Night baseball was coming to New York—another innovation of MacPhail's that the Yankees and Giants thought foolish and unnecessary.

The first night game in New York history was played on June 15, 1938, against the Cincinnati Reds. With a bit of timing that showed that the gods were for the time being on MacPhail's side, pitching for the Reds was a wild, exceedingly quick young left-hander named Johnny Vander Meer, who just four days before had no-hit the Braves.

Fan response to the first night game was overwhelmingly favorable. Too favorable, as a matter of fact. The place was packed, and the fire department finally had to close the gates. MacPhail gave night baseball in Brooklyn a gaudy send-off with a pregame show that included Olympic champion Jesse Owens starring in foot races. But the night proved to belong to Vander Meer, who under Brooklyn's glowing arc lights achieved something that had never been done before, or been done since—a second consecutive no-hitter.

The club finished seventh in 1938, but attendance, stimulated by night baseball, jumped nearly 200,000. There was a new air of optimism and excitement about the ball club now, and the energy center was MacPhail, who knew he had been hired to build a winner and was hell-bent upon doing it.

Not long after the 1938 World Series, Mac-Phail announced that Burleigh Grimes was being let out as manager of the Dodgers. It had been expected. What had not been expected was the name of his replacement, the team's shortstop, Leo Durocher.

MacPhail couldn't have picked a more apt man. Durocher was pure New York, the city where he had begun his big-league career as a utility infielder on the 1928 Yankees. The Massachusetts-born Durocher was always sharp and brash, with an astute baseball mind that had long been apparent. A tactical genius with an abrasive personality that could rub a marble statue raw, Leo was the man to cohere and motivate a team; he would provoke the opposition, arouse the fans, stimulate the press.

Durocher's only real problem in Brooklyn—aside from building a winner—was MacPhail. The stormy personalities and bustling egos of the two men were dangerously similar. Mac-Phail would "fire" Leo countless times over the next few years, but the firings—though quite emphatic at the moment—were so ephemeral that he never even bothered to hire Durocher back. It was MacPhail's way.

70

In 1939 the Dodgers' twin dynamos swung into action. Their early moves did not seem spectacular at first but were to prove extremely shrewd. They drafted a big right-hander from Memphis named Hugh Casey. MacPhail bought from the minor leagues a seemingly washed-up former American League pitcher named Whitlow Wyatt. After a desultory career with the Tigers, White Sox, and Indians, the thirty-two-year-old Wyatt was considered through. Returning to the minors, however, he learned to throw a devastating slider and with it was able to work his way back to the major leagues, with Brooklyn. A gentle, soft-spoken Georgian, Wyatt was a picture of style and grace on the mound, and a more coldblooded competitor never pitched.

In July 1939 MacPhail picked up another supposedly washed-up American Leaguer, an outfielder named Fred (Dixie) Walker. At one time he had been a promising outfielder with the Yankees in the early thirties, but a series of shoulder injuries had curtailed Walker's effectiveness, and he had drifted through the league for several years, always hitting well but apparently injury-prone. MacPhail got him at the waiver price from the Tigers, and Dixie reported to Ebbets Field.

It was love at first sight for Dodger fans. Whatever it is that gives a ball player charisma, Walker surely had it in abundance for the people of Brooklyn. No more popular player ever put on a Dodger uniform. Recognizing the affinity, the writers soon dubbed the new right fielder "The People's Cherce."

The Dodgers finished the '39 season in third place. Attendance jumped to close to a million, and the club was beginning to pay back some of its debts. There was drama and excitement and a certain raucous joy on the grounds at Ebbets Field now. A team was beginning to come together.

In 1938 Branch Rickey was presiding over a vast St. Louis Cardinal farm system that at one time included fifty teams and nearly a thousand players. Rickey had to do a lot of manipulating of contracts to keep all of his players protected. (The Cardinals even had two teams playing in the same league here and there.) Rickey's sharp practices were coming more and more under the intense scrutiny of baseball's stern and unforgiving commissioner, Judge Kenesaw Mountain Landis. Finally exasperated by Rickey's machinations, Landis "liberated" over one hundred players from the Cardinal farm system and gave them free agency.

One of those youngsters, the jewel of the Cardinal organization and the finest young ball player in the land, was a nineteen-year-old from St. Louis named Harold Patrick Reiser, called by one and all "Pistol Pete" because of a youthful affinity for Wild West movies.

It broke Rickey's heart to lose Reiser, who could hit with power from either side of the plate, play infield and outfield with equal skill and zest, and run with blinding speed. MacPhail went after Reiser, gave him a $100 bonus, and signed the handsome kid to a contract. (It later developed that MacPhail had agreed to "hide" the kid in the Dodger farm system for several years and then deal him back to the Cardinals, as a favor to old friend Rickey. Given the dimensions of Reiser's talent, however, it would have been easier to hide the Washington Monument. Pistol Pete was simply too good, and MacPhail had no choice but to renege on the deal.)

Reiser joined the club midway through the 1940 season, the same year the Dodgers acquired a twenty-one-year-old baby-faced shortstop named Harold (Pee Wee) Reese, a youngster of impressive skills and with impeccable baseball instincts born into him.

Reese was playing for Louisville in the American Association, a club then controlled by the Red Sox. Reese was obvious major league material to all who saw him—except Red Sox player-manager Joe Cronin, who just happened to be a shortstop himself. The story was that Cronin, a powerful hitter but mediocre shortstop, was unwilling to move to third to make room for the kid. Cronin was able to impress his opinion on Red Sox owner Tom Yawkey, who promptly sold the youngster to MacPhail. Player-manager Leo Durocher was also a shortstop. When he took one look at Reese, however, he knew his career was over.

Almost manically, MacPhail continued putting together the pieces. On June 12, 1940, he made a startling announcement: The Dodgers had acquired Joe Medwick from the Cardinals for the huge sum of $125,000 and four players. Along with Medwick, the Dodgers obtained a veteran side-wheeling right-hander, Curt Davis.

The twenty-eight-year-old Medwick had been the league's top hitter through the thirties, a right-handed powerhouse who swung at anything and ripped vicious line drives in all directions. Sullen, individualistic, quick with his fists, he was the left fielder the Dodgers needed.

Brooklyn fans were delirious with joy, but not for long. A week after the trade, the Cardinals were in town. With Medwick at the plate, the Cardinal pitcher, right-hander Bob Bowman, let fly a high fastball that Medwick momentarily lost. The ball crashed against his head, and Joe went down and lay sickeningly still.

A moment later pandemonium broke out on the field. The charge was led by Durocher, who claimed the beaning had been deliberate—there was known to be bad blood between Bowman and Medwick.

MacPhail, seething in the press box, later demanded Bowman be barred from baseball for life and tried to have the pitcher indicted for attempted murder. The Cardinals spirited Bowman out of town that night to spare him the wrath of Dodger fans, an excitable species even under normal circumstances.

Medwick recovered—he was back in the lineup in less than a week—but he was never the same hitter again. Lost forever was that aggressive confidence he had always brought to bat with him.

The Dodgers made a run at Cincinnati for the pennant that season, but their tank went dry in late summer. They finished in second place, their highest notch since 1924.

That familiar Brooklyn cry of relentless optimism, "Wait till next year," was to find fulfillment in 1941. It was a long, hard-fought, at times bitter season, with feuds, brawls, spikings, beanball wars. Durocher seemed to go out of his way to antagonize the opposition; Brooklyn was the most hated team in the league, and Leo seemed to prefer it that way.

MacPhail had put the final pieces in place. In need of another starting pitcher, he bought strong-armed, fastballing right-hander Kirby Higbe from the Phillies. In need of a catcher he bought a hustling, battling Mickey Owen from the Cardinals. Only second base remained a problem, and this was taken care of in early May with the purchase of one of the best, Billy Herman, from the Cubs.

The club was now set. It was a marvelously weighed and balanced machine. Camilli was to lead the league in home runs and runs batted in, and ended up being voted Most Valuable Player. What Camilli didn't lead in, Reiser did—doubles, triples, runs scored, slugging average, total bases, batting average. The youngster was proving to be as great as everyone said, and his future seemed unlimited. Reese, playing shortstop like a veteran, Herman at second, and Lavagetto at third gave Brooklyn, along with Camilli, an outstanding infield. Walker and Medwick, flanking Reiser in center field, batted .311 and .318 respectively. Owen was as steady as a rock behind the plate.

The pitching was superb. Wyatt and Higbe topped the league with twenty-two wins each; Curt Davis won thirteen; Hugh Casey, starting and relieving, won fourteen. Thirty-nine-year-old Fred Fitzsimmons, pitching in spots, turned in a 6–1 record.

It was a glorious summer to live in Brooklyn, be a Dodger fan, and have fifty-five cents for a bleacher seat. The battle was waged against a hungry, rugged aggregate of St. Louis Cardinals. These two splendid teams left the rest of the league in shadows as they clawed and scrambled through the season.

On September 25 Wyatt shut out the Braves in Boston, and the pennant was clinched. The final margin was two and a half games. After twenty-one years of wandering in the wilderness, the Dodgers had come home.

Waiting for them in the World Series was a great Yankee team, in the midst of reeling off seven pennants in eight years. The Yankees were led by Joe DiMaggio, who was backed up by Charlie Keller, Bill Dickey, Tommy Henrich, Joe Gordon, and Phil Rizzuto, and although the pitching was not as formidable as the rest of the club, it included steady winners like Red Ruffing, Ernie Bonham, Marius Russo, and Spud Chandler. It was the first of seven World Series meetings between these two clubs over the next fifteen years. One man, Pee Wee Reese, would play in them all.

The first two games were rather quiet and uneventful, Ruffing beating Davis 3–2 in the opener, Wyatt beating Chandler by the same score the next day.

The third game was played at Ebbets Field. Fitzsimmons and Russo dueled tenaciously in a scoreless tie into the top of the seventh. Then a line drive off the bat of Russo struck Fitz on the knee, and he had to leave the game. Casey came in, gave up two runs in the top of the eighth, and Russo held on for a 2–1 win. Brooklyn felt they had gotten a bad break, losing Fitz, who had been hurling so well. But that was nothing compared to what happened the next day, October 5, 1941, destined to stand as the darkest day in Dodger history until Bobby Thomson came to bat in the bottom of the ninth ten years minus two days later.

With Hugh Casey pitching strongly in relief, the Dodgers carried a 4–3 lead into the top of the ninth. Casey retired the first two men easily. The next batter was Tommy Henrich. The count went full. Casey broke off a wicked curve—some say it was a spitter—and Henrich swung and missed. The pitch had so much on it, however, that Owen was unable to hold onto it, and the ball rolled away to the right of the plate. The alert Henrich made it to first. (Owen later claimed that it had not been a spitter but rather the best curveball Casey ever threw. Henrich said the ball "exploded" when it got to the plate and broke with incredible sharpness, to the extent that he was actually trying to check his swing.)

Now Henrich was on first, and Casey was fuming. Instead of going out and talking to his pitcher, as he later conceded he should have, Durocher remained in the dugout, as incredulous as everyone else.

What happened next, in very short order, was brutal. DiMaggio lined a single to left. Keller doubled against the right-field wall for two runs. Dickey walked. Gordon doubled to left for two more runs. It was now 7–4, which was the final score.

The next day—"We couldn't have beaten a girls' team," Billy Herman said ruefully—Bonham allowed but four hits, and the Dodgers went quietly, 3–1, wasting a creditable performance by Wyatt.

By the time the 1942 season rolled around, the country was at war. Cookie Lavagetto joined the Navy, and MacPhail replaced him by swinging a deal with Pittsburgh for their great shortstop Arky Vaughan, who was installed at third base. Otherwise the team was pretty much the same as the year before, perhaps even stronger, with the addition of veteran pitchers Larry French, Johnny Allen, and youngster Ed Head. The team had six winners in double figures and overall won 104 games, enough for a pennant anytime—except in 1942. A relentless Cardinal team was not to be denied, coming from ten and a half behind in August to win 106 games and the pennant.

There was no question but that the Dodgers

lost the pennant on July 19, in St. Louis. With the score tied in the eleventh inning of the second game of a doubleheader, Enos Slaughter hit a shot out to deep center field. Reiser, playing with the reckless zeal that he always did, tracked the ball at top speed and ran full force into the center-field wall. The ball popped out of his glove, and Slaughter circled the bases for a home run. Reiser, hitting nearly .390 at the time, suffered a severe concussion and fractured skull. It was recommended he not play anymore that season. Durocher, however, mesmerized by the youngster's abilities, unwisely reinserted him into the lineup a few days later. But not even Pistol Pete could play with headaches and blurred vision. By season's end his average had shrunk to .310. "I cost us the pennant," Reiser later said. But the guilt lay elsewhere, with Durocher and MacPhail, for letting the youth play. Not only was he costing the team games, but he was probably risking his life. Future injuries, in particular another violent collision with a wall in Brooklyn in 1947, were to sap his blazing talents and deny Pete Reiser a place among the game's immortals. Some starry-eyed romantic later dubbed him "the John Keats of baseball."

The Dodgers had given their fans the two most exciting years in the club's history. But now it was over, and nothing was ever going to be the same again. The nation, indeed the entire world, was falling deeper into the flames of war. After the 1942 season, ball players began entering the armed services in wholesale numbers. Among the first to go were Reese, Reiser, Casey, and French. After the 1943 season, Herman and Higbe went off to war. Vaughan voluntarily retired, and during the '43 season Medwick was dealt to the Giants. Camilli was also dispatched to the Giants in a midseason deal, but Dolph, a Dodger loyalist to the core, retired rather than report.

There was another change after the 1942 season. MacPhail, no doubt feeling the war could not be won without him, resigned from the Dodgers to accept a commission in the Army.

The man chosen to replace MacPhail was Larry's opposite in many ways. Where MacPhail had a flair for the bright lights, gambling, booze, hectic melodrama, Branch Rickey led a quiet, orderly life. Religious, scholarly, a teetotaler, Rickey did not even use profanity, the nearest he came to it being the exclamation, "Judas priest!"

But one thing the two men did have in common was a grim determination to do things their way. Perhaps the most intellectual man ever to come into baseball, Rickey had been a ball player—a poor one—and had managed the Browns and the Cardinals. His biggest impact upon the game, however, had come during his years as general manager of the Cardinals in the twenties and thirties. While he did not invent the farm system, Rickey perfected it. Those were Rickey teams that had made life miserable for Dodger fans these past few years, almost every member of those teams being a homegrown product, signed for a pittance, nurtured through the farm system, and finally brought to the big leagues after undergoing baseball's most exacting winnowing process.

In a tightfisted era, Rickey had the most tenacious grip on a dollar. "He would go into the vault to give you change for a nickel," one of his players said. But he was also the shrewdest appraiser of ball-playing talent ever to squint at a field full of hopefuls.

Rickey's method was to sign any kid who showed a glimmer of talent. In those pre-bonus-player days, youngsters were only too eager to sign a ninety-dollar-a-month contract for the opportunity to play pro ball. When he got to Brooklyn, Rickey continued in this style. He sent his scouts out across the country with orders to sign any likely-looking youngster. He knew that one day the war would be over, and things would return to their proper perspective; when that happened he wanted to have as many of the bright young ball players under contract as he could.

The war years were dismal ones for Brooklyn baseball. Like everyone else, the Dodgers were trying to make do, marking time, filling their roster with shopworn veterans and untried youngsters, most of whom had no business in the major leagues. Baseball was doing its best in response to President Roosevelt's request that the game go on in spite of the war, as a morale builder for the nation and its servicemen.

The Dodgers had a few bona fide big leaguers during those dreary years, including Eddie Stanky, Augie Galan, Curt Davis, and Dixie Walker, who helped lift the gloom with a batting championship in 1944, hitting .357. In 1944 forty-one-year-old Paul Waner played alongside sixteen-year-old Tommy Brown and seventeen-year-old Eddie Miksis. In 1945 a caretaker of Brooklyn's past, Babe Herman, was brought

out of retirement and employed as a pinch hitter. The forty-two-year-old Babe hit a respectable .265. Among the many young faces that ducked in and out of Brooklyn during the war years was nineteen-year-old Gil Hodges, who went zero for two in 1943 before going off to war.

In 1943 they finished third. In 1944, with fifty-three different men in uniform at one time or another, they finished seventh. In 1945 they were third.

The war ended in the summer of '45. Baseball was looking ahead to 1946, hoping to pick up where it left off in 1942. But it was not going to be business as usual. Branch Rickey had already seen to that. The sixty-four-year-old boss of the Dodgers was about to drag the conservative old game screaming and kicking into a new era.

For a while he looked like the real thing. Ernie Koy could run like the blazes, and in his rookie year of 1938 the powerfully built outfielder hit .299, higher than any other regular. He dropped to .278 the next year, then in June 1940 was sent to St. Louis as part of the Medwick deal.

Johnny Hudson was a utility infielder for the Dodgers from 1936–40. The only time he played a full season was 1938, when he batted .261.

They called him "Blimp," but only because it was easier to spell than dirigible. But put a bat in his hands, and Babe Phelps was a heavy bomber. A catcher for the Dodgers from 1935–41, Phelps did his heaviest bombing in 1936, when he hit .367 in 115 games. He followed that heady year with averages of .313 and .308. But Babe was moody. He didn't like to fly. He didn't like Larry MacPhail. And sometimes he didn't feel like playing. When Mickey Owen joined the team in 1941 there was no longer any need to pamper the big guy, and Babe was suspended. He was traded to Pittsburgh after the season.

Freddie Fitzsimmons in 1926.

Luke Hamlin pitched for Brooklyn from 1937–41. In 1939 he surprised everyone by winning twenty and losing thirteen. That banner season proved to be totally out of character, however, and when Luke started throwing long balls, Leo soured on him.

76

Larry MacPhail in 194

Harry "Cookie" Lavagetto in 1938.

Walter (Red) Barber, probably the finest broadcaster of baseball games ever to sit behind a microphone. From 1939 until 1953, when he went to work for the Yankees, Barber's warm, witty, and literate reporting and commentary brought the adventures of the Brooklyn Dodgers into living rooms, saloons, barbershops, automobiles, and anywhere else a radio could be found in greater New York. For fifteen years he made the Dodgers and Ebbets Field vivid, picturesque, exciting, and important. He was a phrasemaker: a "rhubarb" was a squabble on the field; a lot of runs scored meant they were "tearin' up the pea-patch"; when the bases were "FOB" you knew there was a Dodger on each one; somebody was "as mad as a bear with a boil in its nose." And so on. Behind the down-home colloquialisms, however, was quite an erudite and well-read Southern gentleman.

78

Dolph Camilli in 1938.

MacPhail and Dodger coach Babe Ruth, in 1938. In an effort to hype attendance, MacPhail hired Ruth to coach first base. (Shockingly, baseball could find no employment for Ruth at that time.) Babe wasn't much of a coach, undependable when it came to remembering signs. His primary job, however, was to take batting practice, and many fans came early to watch the Babe's still flawless swing rocket baseballs out into Bedford Avenue.

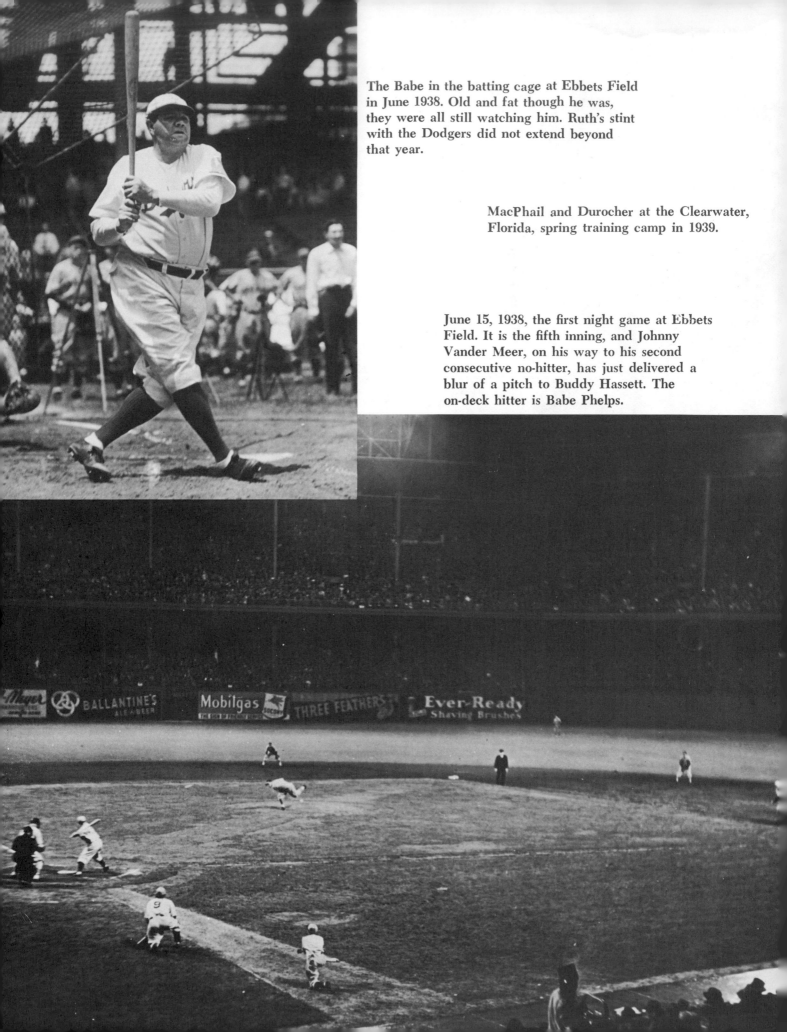

The Babe in the batting cage at Ebbets Field in June 1938. Old and fat though he was, they were all still watching him. Ruth's stint with the Dodgers did not extend beyond that year.

MacPhail and Durocher at the Clearwater, Florida, spring training camp in 1939.

June 15, 1938, the first night game at Ebbets Field. It is the fifth inning, and Johnny Vander Meer, on his way to his second consecutive no-hitter, has just delivered a blur of a pitch to Buddy Hassett. The on-deck hitter is Babe Phelps.

Leo Durocher as a Yankee rookie in 1928.

John Whitlow Wyatt in 1939.

July 26, 1938, at Ebbets Field. The Cubs' Stan Hack comes safely into third base, while Lavagetto awaits a throw that never came.

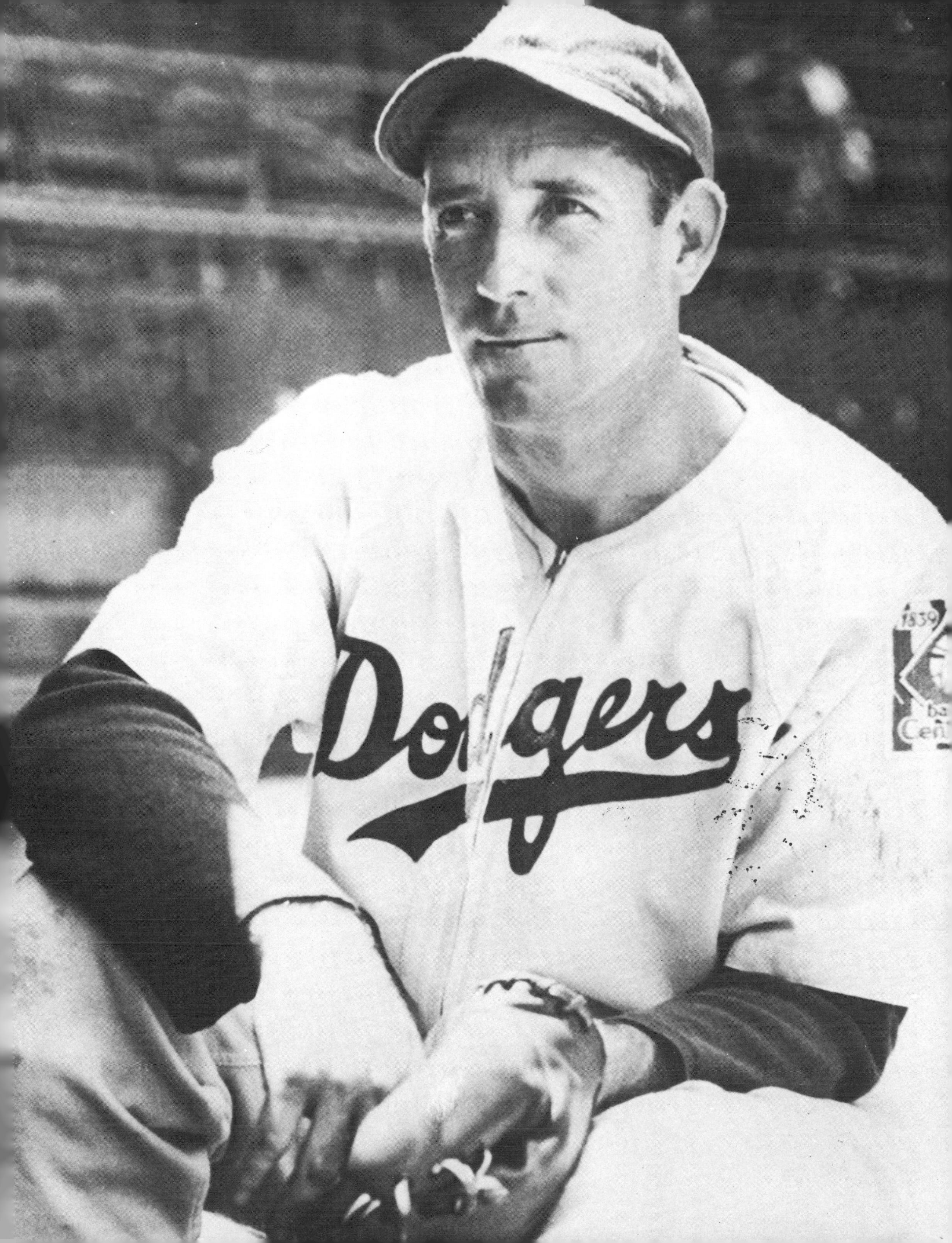
Dodgers
1839

The People's Cherce in 1939.

Dixie Walker as a Yankee hopeful in 1935.

It is 1939, and this young man, just twenty years old and a total stranger to all, has appeared at the Clearwater camp. Leo is letting him work out with the big boys as a favor to an old friend. The young man's name is Pete Reiser. The exhibition games start, and Leo, who has taken a liking to the kid, lets him play. Pete gets on base eleven consecutive times, including a couple of home runs off Lefty Gomez and Tommy Bridges. Pete Reiser ceases to be a stranger.

Pete Coscarart played second base for the Dodgers from 1938–41, until Billy Herman showed up.

Formerly a top pitcher with the Cardinals and Cubs, Tex Carleton was on the way down when the Dodgers took a chance on him in 1940. The thirty-four-year-old Texan was only 6–6 and didn't finish the year, but on April 30 he surprised everybody by no-hitting the Cincinnati Reds.

Pee Wee Reese in 1940.

Joe Medwick.

June 18, 1940. Joe Medwick, a $125,000 investment who has been a Brooklyn Dodger for about a week, has just been beaned by ex-teammate Bob Bowman. Good and beaned. Joe is out cold. The fact that Joe's feet are still on the spot where he had been standing indicates that he just keeled over like a felled tree, probably unconscious before he hit the ground. The catcher, who looks as though he is holding his cap solemnly over his heart, is Walker Cooper. Even the umpire looks as though he is tipping his cap farewell to Joe. Leo Durocher, number two, has catapulted from the dugout to home plate.

It is September 7, 1940, at Ebbets Field. Phillies pitcher Kirby Higbe has just hit Medwick with a pitch. Joe has had just about enough of this and wants to bend his bat on Kirby's head. Kirby, a tough monkey, is ready to take on Joe, bat and all. Leo and Umpire Babe Pinelli are the agents of restraint. Catcher Bennie Warren is taking it all in. A year later Medwick and Higbe were teammates, fighting the world as one.

A classic moment at Ebbets Field. It is September 1940, and Umpire George Magerkurth, never a particular favorite in Brooklyn, finds himself in a postgame discussion about some of his decisions with a loyal Dodger fan. Umpire Bill Stewart, coming up from the rear, hauled the fan off of Big George, and the police did the rest. The fan bought himself some time in the slammer for his trouble.

Kirby Higbe in 1941. MacPhail ransomed him from the Phillies for $100,000.

Mickey Owen. The Cardinals charged $55,000 for him.

In the spring of 1941 this was the Dodger infield. Left to right, utility man Lew Riggs, shortstop Pee Wee Reese, second baseman Pete Coscarart, third baseman Cookie Lavagetto, first baseman Dolph Camilli.

Billy Herman was acquired from the Cubs early in May to play second base. A deadly clutch hitter, a superb hit-and-run man, and an excellent fielder, he gave the Dodgers one classy infield.

Hugh Casey in 1941.

The babies of the '41 Dodgers: Reiser, left, and Reese.

Reese and Medwick in 1941.

The saga of Pete Reiser—power at the plate,
excitement on the bases, and injuries. Pete
is being carried off the field after being
beaned by the Phillies' Ike Pearson in
Brooklyn in April 1941.

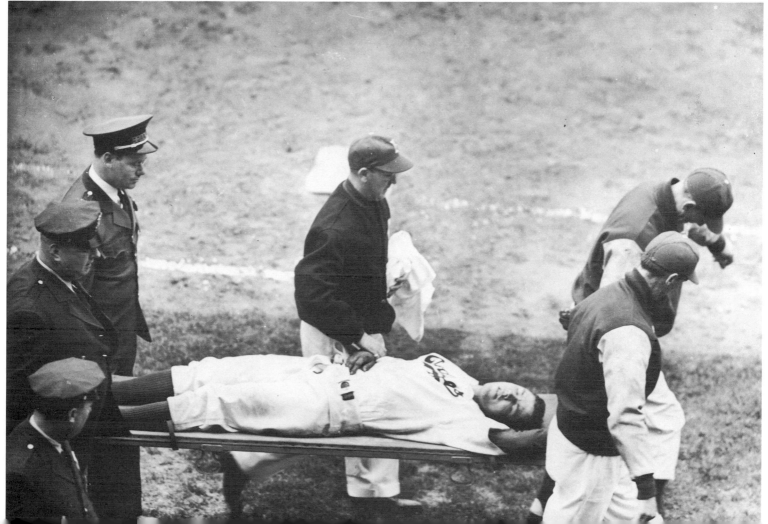

Curt Davis was a throw-in in the Medwick deal, but he proved to be a valuable pitcher for the Dodgers. He was 13–7 in the pennant year, 15–6 the next year. Curt pitched for the Dodgers until 1946.

September 14, 1941, at St. Louis, and the pennant race is blazing. Brooklyn is one game ahead of St. Louis. Durocher is disputing Umpire Babe Pinelli's decision that a Whit Wyatt pitch struck Estel Crabtree on the foot. Gathered around the two debaters are, left to right, Lew Riggs, Dolph Camilli, catcher Herman Franks, and the next batter, Frank Crespi. This game, which Brooklyn won, was the classic Dodger-Cardinal game of the early forties. Wyatt outpitched Cardinal ace Mort Cooper, 1–0. Cooper had a no-hitter going into the top of the eighth, when Dixie Walker and Billy Herman suddenly hit back-to-back doubles for the game's only run. Breathing hard, the Dodgers left St. Louis with a two-game lead and were never headed.

Aerial view of Ebbets Field, September 1941.

The Dodgers obtained outfielder Jimmy Wasdell from the Washington Senators in 1940, and Jimmy gave them good service as a utility outfielder. He batted .298 in 1941.

Durocher and Fitzsimmons in 1941.

It is September 25, 1941, and Whitlow Wyatt, right, has just clinched Brooklyn's first pennant in twenty-one years by shutting out the Braves in Boston. Durocher is hugging his ace. On the left is Fred Fitzsimmons.

Medwick, Herman, Reese, Reiser, Owen, and Wyatt lined up in the dugout at Ebbets Field, September 1941.

It is September 2, 1941, and the streets of Brooklyn belong to the Dodgers. MacPhail and Durocher are spearheading the caravan. The Bill Terry sign on the left indicates that Dodger fans have long memories.

Opposing pitchers for the second game of the 1941 World Series: Whitlow Wyatt, left, and the Yankees' Spud Chandler.

Lavagetto scoring in seventh inning of first game, at Yankee Stadium. The catcher is Bill Dickey, the umpire Bill McGowan. Number eight is Dixie Walker.

98

It's the fourth inning of the second game, and Billy Herman, having just forced Joe Gordon at second, is firing to first base trying to double up Spud Chandler. Spud was safe.

Freddie Fitzsimmons, Leo's surprise starter for game three.

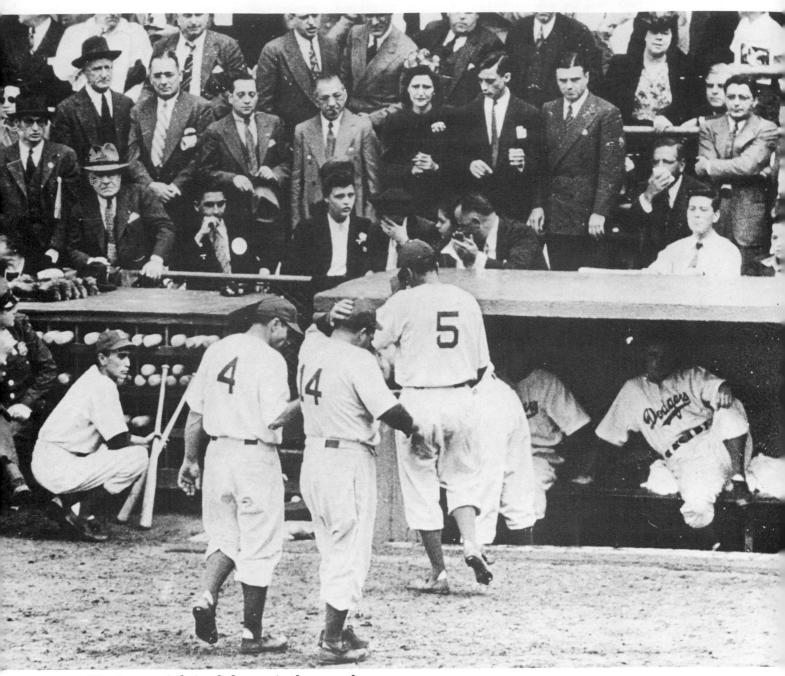

Fitzsimmons is being led away in the seventh
inning after being struck on the kneecap
by Russo's line drive. Mrs. Fitzsimmons can
be seen sitting right behind the dugout, her
hand covering her face.

The incredible has just happened. A frantic
Owen is going after the dropped third strike,
the alert Henrich is off to first base, Umpire
Larry Goetz is signaling that it is strike
three.

A few moments later Joe DiMaggio is sliding
home with what proved to be the winning
run on Keller's belt against the right-field
wall. Number seven is Tommy Henrich, who
has just scored the tying run.

Dolph Camilli showing off the watch he received for being voted the National League's Most Valuable Player in 1941.

Young Ed Head was a pleasant pitching surprise for the Dodgers in 1942, with a 10–6 record. He entered the service during the 1944 season. Returning in 1946, he started off well, pitching a no-hitter against the Braves on April 23. Soon after, however, the right-hander came up with a sore arm, which ended his career.

Larry French in 1942. The Dodgers obtained this smooth, veteran left-hander from the Cubs at the tail end of the '41 season. In 1942 Larry pitched great ball for Brooklyn, winning fifteen and losing only four, with an ERA of 1.83. The thirty-five-year-old French then joined the Navy and never returned to baseball, opting instead for a second career in the Navy, where he remained for twenty-five years, retiring with the rank of captain.

If Johnny Allen looks mean and tough, well, he was. After a brilliant career in the American League, the tempestuous right-hander joined the Dodgers late in the 1941 season. In 1942 the thirty-eight-year-old Allen was 10–6. Always difficult to handle, he was sent to the Giants the next year.

Arky Vaughan, whom the Dodgers obtained from Pittsburgh after the 1941 season. To get Arky they gave up Luke Hamlin, Babe Phelps, Pete Coscarart, and Jimmy Wasdell. Vaughan, after Honus Wagner probably the greatest shortstop in National League history, was installed at third base to replace Lavagetto, who had joined the Navy. Not even the great Vaughan could displace Reese at shortstop. Arky played for the Dodgers in 1942–43, retired for three years, then returned for two years in 1947. Vaughan's absence from the Hall of Fame remains Cooperstown's number-one scandal.

It is May 8, 1942, and a packed house is watching the flag-raising ceremony prior to a twilight game between the Dodgers and Giants. The Dodger players are lined up along the right-field foul line. Proceeds from the game were donated to the Navy Relief Fund.

Dixie Walker churns up the dust as he slides across home plate on an inside-the-park home run against the Braves at Ebbets Field on May 31, 1942. The catcher is Clyde Kluttz.

The stylish form of Whitlow Wyatt. Whit was 19–7 in 1942.

Some of the Cardinals who helped St. Louis outrace Brooklyn for the pennant in 1942. Left to right, first baseman Ray Sanders, catcher Walker Cooper, pitcher Mort Cooper, outfielder Enos (Country) Slaughter.

Augie Galan was considered by some to be washed up when the Dodgers acquired him from the Cubs during the 1941 season. Augie fooled them all and played good ball for Brooklyn through 1946. A sharp-hitting outfielder, Augie's best years were 1944–46, when he hit .318, .307, and .310.

Major Larry MacPhail and Leo Durocher in 1944.

The thirty-three-year-old manager of the St. Louis Browns, Branch Rickey, in 1914.

First baseman Howie Schultz was brought up during the 1943 season. He was supposed to make Dodger fans forget Dolph Camilli. He didn't. The 6′ 6″ Schultz stayed with Brooklyn until 1947. His most memorable moment as a Dodger is a negative one: with the Dodgers trailing 8–4 and the bases loaded with two out in the ninth inning of the second playoff game against the Cardinals in 1946, Howie struck out.

Branch Rickey in 1960.

Bobo Newsom played for just about every-body else, so it was inevitable that at one time or another he would stop by and get into a Dodger uniform. The time was at the end of the 1942 season, when Brooklyn obtained him from Washington to help during the stretch run. Bobo was 2–2 that fall. He was 9–4 halfway through the next season when he had a falling-out with Durocher. Since Bobo was traded nine times during his big-league career, perhaps the disagreement wasn't entirely Leo's fault. A little-known fact about Bobo is that he first came to the big leagues with Brooklyn, back in 1929. That year he was 0–3 with a 10.61 ERA. But Bobo would improve with age.

Art Herring, shown here in 1934 when he pitched briefly for the Dodgers, came back to help out during the war years. He stayed on through 1946, at the age of thirty-nine giving the team some splendid relief pitching and a W–L record of 7–2.

Gene Mauch, who was with the Dodgers for a short time in 1944 and again in 1948, later went on to become a longtime, highly respected big-league manager.

In 1944 Dodger fans were startled to hear that they now had a new young pitcher with the awesome name of Calvin Coolidge Julius Caesar Tuskahoma McLish. Cal was 3–10 that year and then went off to war. Years later Cal (whom Kirby Higbe called "Herbert Hoover") was to have some winning seasons for Cleveland, but for Dodger fans he will always be, so to speak, just a name.

It is 1944, the bleakest of the war years for baseball. The teams are scrambling desperately for ball-playing talent. The Dodgers have signed up Ben Chapman (left), a washed-up former American League outfielder, as a pitcher; and sixteen-year-old Tommy Brown, a shortstop. Brown, who hit .164 in forty-six games in 1944, later carved out a modest big-league career for himself, playing for the Dodgers until 1951 before being traded to Philadelphia. Standing in the middle, smiling bravely, is Manager Durocher.

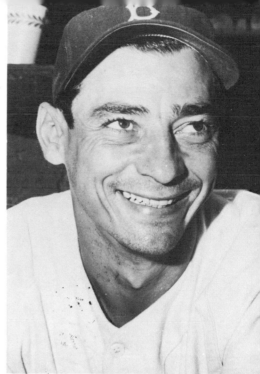

Luis Olmo joined the Dodgers in 1943 and hit .303. In 1945 the Puerto Rican outfielder-third baseman batted .313 and led the league with thirteen triples. In 1946 Olmo and some other big leaguers jumped to the Mexican League which had been organized by the wealthy Pasqual brothers, who were trying to entice big-league ball players south of the border with large sums of money. Mickey Owen was another Dodger who succumbed. The Mexican League crumbled after several years, and in 1949 the players began returning, Olmo among them. Luis helped out in the '49 pennant drive, batting .305 as a part-timer. He was traded to the Braves the next year.

Goody Rosen was in the Dodger outfield in the late thirties without any particular distinction. He returned as a wartime replacement in 1944, batting .261. The next year, however, Goody generated a lot of Ebbets Field excitement when he hit .325 and challenged for the batting crown until a late-season tail-off took him out of the race. He was traded to the Giants early in 1946.

Vic Lombardi, a little left-hander, pitched for the Dodgers from 1945–47, compiling a three-year record of 35–32. He is shown here in the spring of 1945 at Bear Mountain, New York, where, because of wartime travel restrictions, the Dodgers did their spring training.

Paul Waner, one of the greatest hitters in National League history, was forty years old when he played for Brooklyn in the wartime year of 1943. Nevertheless, Paul's bat was still quick enough to hit .311. He was released the following September after batting .287.

Chapter 6

The Glorious Decade

ON OCTOBER 23, 1945, Rickey called the press to the Dodger team office for the purpose of making an announcement. It was a startling announcement: The Brooklyn Dodgers had signed to a contract with their Montreal farm club a twenty-six-year-old Negro infielder named Jackie Robinson. Rickey, to the chagrin of his fellow owners, many players, and certain segments of the press, had broken a barrier that had been erected and maintained throughout baseball history by that most infamous bit of architecture—a gentleman's agreement.

For all the years he had been in baseball, Rickey had been brooding about the exclusion of black Americans from America's favorite game. The policy was unfair, unjust, prejudicial, illegal, and disgraceful. But it wasn't until after the war that Rickey felt confident enough to make his move at last. And with equal confidence, he felt he had found the right man with whom to make the move.

Rickey needed more than just a great ball player; he also needed a man of great intelligence, a man with a sense of history. He needed a man of paradoxical qualities—one with burning competitive fires who would not respond to insult or indignity. One racially inspired fight on the field could set back the "cause"—as Rickey referred to his great idea—for a decade or more. A very special man was needed. Jack Roosevelt Robinson was precisely that man. Playing under conditions that no athlete, before or since, has ever had to endure, Robinson transcended baseball and stepped into American history.

Born in Georgia, Robinson grew up in California. After an outstanding athletic career at UCLA he entered the Army and rose to the rank of lieutenant. When he left the service he joined the Kansas City Monarchs, a black professional team. It was while playing with the Monarchs in 1945 that Rickey had him scouted.

So sensitive was Rickey's plan that he confided his true intentions to no one. The Dodger scouts who were appraising Robinson (and other blacks) for Rickey were under the impression that the old man was planning to organize a black team to play in Ebbets Field when the Dodgers were on the road.

The resistance to Robinson was mountainous. Rickey's fellow club owners were unanimous in their condemnation of the move. Nor were some of the Dodger players pleased about it. When Jackie was promoted to the Dodgers in April 1947, after a spectacularly successful year with Montreal, there was some grumbling in Dodger ranks.

There were also some pragmatic souls on the club who, having lost the pennant in 1946 in a playoff, set but one criterion for the new man: Can he help us win (ergo, make money)? The question would be answered shortly, and dramatically.

The Dodgers and Cardinals had picked up in 1946 where they left off in 1942, fighting a bruising, overheated pennant race that ended in a tie on the last day of the season. Baseball's first pennant playoff followed, according to National League rules a two-out-of-three series. The Cardinals took it in two straight.

The '46 team was a mix of old and new. Reese, Lavagetto, Casey, Reiser, and Higbe were back, and among the new faces the most notable was a twenty-four-year-old outfielder named Carl Furillo, who hit .284 in his rookie year and possessed a cannonlike throwing arm. In mid-season Rickey had traded Billy Herman and his high salary to the Braves, a move that probably cost Brooklyn the pennant.

Robinson was officially promoted to the Dodgers on opening day in 1947. While Jackie's move had been expected by many, what had occurred the week before was not: Brooklyn had lost its manager to a year's suspension, so ordered by Commissioner Albert B. (Happy)

Chandler, a Kentucky politician who had become baseball's second commissioner after the death of Judge Landis.

Durocher had become caught in the cross fire between two of the game's strongest personalities, Rickey and Larry MacPhail, back from the wars and now running the Yankees. It began when Leo took a few swipes at MacPhail in a ghost-written newspaper column carrying Leo's byline. MacPhail blasted back, Rickey answered, and the whole thing quickly blew out of proportion. To complicate the situation, Leo was on thin ice with Chandler because of Leo's predilection for the high life and alleged associations with gamblers and other unsavory types. When Durocher was further charged with hobnobbing with a couple of known gamblers during a Dodger-Yankee exhibition game in Havana, Chandler lowered the boom. "As a result of the accumulation of unpleasant incidents in which he has been involved which the commissioner construes as detrimental to baseball," Chandler's decision read, "Manager Durocher is hereby suspended from participating in professional baseball for the 1947 season."

There is no question but that Durocher was dealt with with gross unfairness in this situation. He had done nothing wrong and was hardly detrimental to baseball; if anything, Leo was one of the game's glossier assets. It is quite possible that Chandler was trying to establish himself as a strong commissioner in the Landis tradition. In any event, Happy was not perceived as a success by the owners, and after one term in the job his contract was not renewed.

In desperate need of a manager now—Jackie Robinson and a new season were just a week away—Rickey first aproached Joe McCarthy, who had resigned from the Yankees the year before. McCarthy was not interested. The season opened with coach Clyde Sukeforth running the club as interim manager. Rickey finally brought in to manage an old and trusted friend, Burt Shotton, then a troubleshooter in the Dodger organization.

The sixty-two-year-old Shotton, a rather reserved, good-natured man, had played for Rickey when Branch was managing the Browns around the time of the First World War. A .270 lifetime hitter, Shotton's career had been steady if undistinguished. After his playing career ended he had managed the Phillies for six years, from 1928–33. Dodger fans seldom caught a glimpse of their new skipper, since Burt never suited up, preferring to manage from the dugout wearing civvies. But he was just the man to steer a very volatile ship through a stormy and hectic season.

It was true that once the Dodgers saw Robinson play ball, a lot, though not all, of the dissension disappeared. But there was trouble from the opposition, most dramatically when the Dodgers encountered the Cardinals for the first time. Some of the Redbirds threatened to strike rather than appear on the field with a black man. This was a pretty hot situation, and into the middle of it stepped National League President Ford Frick. Normally a rather uninspiring man, personification of the highly conservative baseball establishment, Frick suddenly became a lion. He issued a ringing statement that threatened suspension for all who struck, and damn the consequences. "This is the United States of America," the angry Frick declared, apparently feeling it necessary to remind the few fractious Cardinals of this fact (and they were few in number), "and one citizen has as much right to play as another."

There was no strike.

Under Shotton's steady hand, the Dodgers, led by Robinson, charged through the league and came in five games ahead of the Cardinals.

This Dodger team was the beginning of the greatest era in Brooklyn baseball history, set to win six pennants in ten years. It was going to become one of the most powerful teams of all time. Some of the men were already there—Robinson, Reese, Furillo, and two youngsters who saw limited action in 1947, Duke Snider and Gil Hodges, then still considered a catcher. And in the vast Dodger farm system were others, including Roy Campanella and Don Newcombe. (Few major league clubs had so far followed Rickey's lead in signing blacks, and the vast talent pool was still almost exclusively Brooklyn's. Rickey's dedication to the "cause" was still intense. With an opportunity to sign young Larry Doby, Rickey passed when he heard Bill Veeck wanted Doby for the Indians. Thus, Doby became the first black to play in the American League.)

Robinson's rookie year was remarkable in many ways. Not only was he a lone figure, unable to register in many hotels around the country, but he was subject to almost constant abuse, torment, and humiliation. Also, he had been posted to an unfamiliar position—first base—in order to fill a void. Eddie Stanky was at second, rookie John (Spider) Jorgensen was at third, and in the outfield along with Furillo was the veteran Walker and an injury-plagued Reiser. Young Ralph Branca led the pitchers with twenty-one victories, followed by lefty Joe Hatten's seventeen. Casey was still king of the bullpen. Kirby Higbe, uncomfortable on the same team as Robinson, had been traded to the Pirates early in the year for a barrel of money and a little outfielder named Al Gionfriddo.

It was another Yankee-Dodger World Series that fall, and true to the pattern of Brooklyn World Series appearances, there was one extremely bizarre game. This time, however, calamity's fallout landed on the other side of the fence.

The Series started off typically enough, with the Yankees winning the first two games. The Dodgers bounced back and took a rather wild game three by a 9–8 score.

Game four was played at Ebbets Field on October 3. The opposing pitchers were Harry

Taylor for the Dodgers and a journeyman right-hander, Floyd (Bill) Bevens, for the Yankees. Over the season, for a pennant-winning club, Bevens had posted a mediocre 7–13 record. Yankee manager Bucky Harris had seen his staff pretty well chewed up in the previous day's slugfest, hence the selection of Bevens.

Taylor, who had had an excellent rookie season for the Dodgers, came into the Series with a sore arm. Starting him was a gamble. A bad gamble—he never got out of the first inning. Only some heroic relief pitching by Hal Gregg held the Yankees to one run. In the fourth the Yankees scored again. In the bottom of the fifth the Dodgers got one back without benefit of a base hit. So it was 2–1.

Bevens was pitching a very peculiar game. Through eight innings he nursed along his slim margin without yielding a hit, but he had surrendered eight bases on balls. In the top of the ninth Hugh Casey relieved with one out and the bases loaded, threw one pitch and got Tommy Henrich (remember them from the '41 Series?) to bounce into a double play. That neat bit by Casey has been forgotten, but it proved to be crucial, in light of what happened a few minutes later.

Walking out to the mound to pitch the bottom of the ninth, Bevens was three outs away from pitching the first World Series no-hitter. Thirty-three thousand fans—most of them of Dodger blood—were ranting and raving, pleading with their boys to prevent this ultimate humiliation. (The perfect game in the World Series hadn't been invented yet. Little did they know!)

Bevens retired the first hitter, Bruce Edwards, on a fly to DiMaggio in deep center. Carl Furillo drew Bevens' ninth walk. Spider Jorgensen fouled to George McQuinn behind first base. Two out. Shotton inserted Al Gionfriddo in to run for Furillo, then sent Pete Reiser up to bat for Casey. Pete was out of the lineup with a broken ankle, but such was Shot-

ton's faith in this great player that he sent him up nevertheless. Yankee manager Bucky Harris was to show even greater faith when, after Gionfriddo stole second, he broke one of baseball's commanding axioms and ordered Reiser walked, thus putting the winning run on base. Broken ankle or no broken ankle, Harris did not want Pete swinging that lethal bat. Eddie Miksis was sent in to run for Reiser. Shotton, playing a hot hand now, sent the veteran Cookie Lavagetto up to bat for Stanky.

Cookie responded with a line drive that, on quiet nights in Brooklyn, can still be heard humming and whistling. The ball hit low off the right-field wall. Henrich had a moment's trouble judging the ball's trajectory, another moment of trouble picking it up, and by the time the throw came home Gionfriddo had scored, Miksis was lying in a cloud of dust on home plate, Mickey Owen had been avenged, and Bevens was walking disconsolately from the field while the whole world—it seemed like the whole world, anyway—was trying joyously to tear pieces from the body of Cookie Lavagetto.

The Yankees, however, were unimpressed. They recovered and took the Series in seven games. The last blaze of excitement occurred in game six, at Yankee Stadium, when defensive replacement Gionfriddo made a spectacular running grab of a tremendous clout by DiMaggio which helped Brooklyn win the game.

It was in some ways an ironic World Series. The great stars, the DiMaggios, the Henrichs, the Reeses, the Robinsons, had been upstaged by destiny's irregulars—Bevens, Lavagetto, Gionfriddo. Tradition had the last word, though: not Bevens or Lavagetto or Gionfriddo ever appeared in another major league game.

Leo was back in '48, and Shotton retired from the dugout. Meanwhile, a few more faces had been added to the squad. On December 8, 1947, Rickey had swung a trade with the Pirates. Trade is the polite word. One almost has to believe Rickey was holding a gun in his hand while he engineered this transaction. From the Dodgers went the thirty-seven-year-old Walker, a fading People's Cherce; left-hander Vic Lombardi, a .500 pitcher who was soon to exit from the scene; and right-hander Hal Gregg, who was to win exactly three games for the Pirates. In return the Dodgers got Billy Cox, perhaps the greatest fielding third baseman of all time (there surely has been none better), and left-hander Elwyn "Preacher" Roe. To give some idea of Rickey's beagle nose for talent, one has only to examine the thirty-three-year-old Roe's record for the previous two years: seven wins and twenty-three losses. Over the next seven years this canny left-hander was to win ninety-three for the Dodgers and lose just thirty-seven.

By the end of the '48 season the great team which was to dominate the National League for the next decade had taken shape. Gil Hodges was now the first baseman, Robinson was at second, Reese at short, Cox at third. Furillo was in right field, Snider in center, while left field was always destined to be patrolled by transients. Roy Campanella, brought up in mid-season after being sent in the spring to the American Association as the first black in that league ("I ain't no pioneer," Campy had grumbled to Rickey), was behind the plate.

The pitching staff was crowded with hard-throwing youngsters of immense promise, like Ralph Branca (already a twenty-game winner), Erv Palica, Jack Banta, and the fastest of them all, Rex Barney, who could throw a ball through that proverbial brick wall that baseball erects every time a Rex Barney makes an appearance. There were also the craftsmen, like Roe and Carl Erskine.

The year turned out to be a transitional one, however, and the team finished third, seven and a half games behind the Braves. The most startling occurrence of 1948 concerned Leo Durocher. After several months it became apparent that Leo's once close relationship with Rickey had deteriorated. Soon after the all-star game an astonishing announcement was made: Mel Ott, manager of the Giants and a Polo Grounds idol of some twenty years' standing, had been let out. His replacement was the hated Leo Durocher, eased out of Brooklyn by Rickey.

It was a bitter pill for Giant fans, but one of the smartest moves Giants' owner Horace Stoneham ever made. The likable Ott was dull; the Giants were dull. Leo Durocher was many things; dull was not one of them. Dodger fans were astonished more than upset; Leo had never been a particular hero in Ebbets Field (to his credit, however, Leo never wanted to be a hero anywhere—he only wanted to win).

Burt Shotton returned and quietly led the team to a third-place finish.

The following year found the Dodgers outracing a familiar opponent down to the wire. They clinched the pennant on the last day of the season, finishing one game ahead of the Cardinals. The race was close all the way. From August 20 to September 29 the Dodgers were in second place, always one or two nerve-racking games behind. Then they squeezed in by a game and held on to the end, winning in ten innings in Philadelphia on the season's last day. Reliever Jack Banta was the hero, pitching four and a third innings of shutout ball.

Robinson had his greatest year in '49, leading the league with a .342 average and being voted the league's Most Valuable Player. Duke Snider, in his first full season, batted .292 with 23 home runs. In his first full season at first base, Gil Hodges drove in 115 runs. Young Don Newcombe was brought up from Montreal in May and went on to a 17–8 record.

Newcombe's promotion should have come earlier, but the team was concerned about the young man's volatile temperament. Newk had a tendency to pop off. Shotton was afraid Newcombe might "spoil it for the other two fellows," meaning Campanella, always a moderate sort, and Robinson, who was still keeping the lid on his fire. Rickey's social experiment on the base-ball diamond was still on trial.

At this time the only other black players in the league were the Giants' Monte Irvin and Henry Thompson. What the other clubs were waiting for—or hoping for—is left to speculation.

The World Series that year—against the Yankees, of course—was a quiet one. The Yankees took it in five, with Preacher Roe's 1–0 victory in the second game the only bright spot. The opening game featured a classic pitching duel between two fastballing right-handers, Newcombe and the Yankees' Allie Reynolds. They went into the bottom of the ninth in a scoreless game. Newk fell behind two balls and no strikes on leadoff hitter Tommy Henrich. Henrich set himself for a fastball. He got it. The moment Newcombe heard the crack of the bat, he put his glove in his pocket and strode off the mound without looking back. He knew.

The Dodgers were the overwhelming favorite to repeat in 1950, and they did lead the league in hits, home runs, runs, batting, and slugging. Despite all of this power, the club finished second to the Phillies, who took their first pennant since 1915.

The Dodgers were undone by a shaky pitching staff. Newcombe and Roe each won nineteen, young Erv Palica won thirteen, but after that the wins were hard to come by. Jack Banta had a sore arm, Branca couldn't win, fireballer Rex Barney couldn't find the strike zone. Even so, the Brooks weren't out of it until the tenth inning of the season finale at Ebbets Field.

On September 19 the Dodgers had trailed the Phillies—this was their "Whiz Kid" team—by nine games. On October 1 the two clubs were in Brooklyn, playing a game that could throw them into a deadlock if the Dodgers won it, necessitating a playoff.

The Phillies' collapse was traceable to injuries to two key pitchers, Bob Miller and Bubba Church, and the loss of star left-hander Curt Simmons to the Army in mid-September. The Philadelphia pitching staff virtually started and ended with Robin Roberts and relief ace Jim Konstanty.

Don Newcombe found himself in another memorable pitching duel that Sunday, opposed by the great Roberts, making his third start in five days. The score was 1–1 in the bottom of the ninth, and Cal Abrams opened with a walk. Reese singled him to second. With the Phillies looking for a bunt, Shotton let Snider swing away, and the Duke lined a hard single to center. Too hard, probably, because Richie Ashburn came in quickly, picked it up, and threw Abrams out at the plate by a wide margin.

That left runners on second and third, one out, and Robinson up. Jackie was intentionally walked, filling the bases. But Carl Furillo popped out, and Gil Hodges flied out.

In the top of the tenth, Dick Sisler came up with two on and hit a wrong-field, line-drive home run into the lower stands in left. The final score was 4–1.

The end of the 1950 season allowed the club's top management to focus on the struggle for control of the team, a struggle which had been intensifying throughout the summer. In 1945 the heirs of Charles Ebbets and Ed McKeever had divested themselves of their stock, a combined holding of around 75 percent. For a price of a little over one million dollars, three men bought equal shares in the club. They were Branch Rickey, a business executive named John Smith, and a lawyer named Walter O'Malley. Smith soon died, and O'Malley, who had joined the club in 1943 as its attorney, took over his stock.

O'Malley and Rickey, two strong and highly intelligent men, were never comfortable with one another. Finally, in 1950, Rickey sold out his interest to O'Malley at a huge profit and departed to become general manager of the Pittsburgh Pirates. The shrewd, ambitious, manipulative O'Malley was now principal owner and president of the Brooklyn Dodgers.

117

O'Malley's first move was to hire a new manager, replacing Shotton. The new man was Charlie Dressen. Dressen was a familiar face, having been Durocher's third-base coach for many years. Previously, Charlie had been a third baseman for Cincinnati and later managed the club for MacPhail. When MacPhail took over the Yankees in 1947, Dressen became a coach there.

Dressen was one of the sharpest baseball men who ever lived. He was a short, smiling, ebullient optimist, with a genius for stealing the opposition's signs. He was also something of an egomaniac. One of his favorite comments to his players was, "Stay close till the eighth inning, and I'll think of something." That ego was buried in a personality so chipper, however, that Charlie was always popular with his men, who often were in awe of his keen baseball sense.

Dressen got his machinelike team off to a fast start in 1951. The '51 Dodgers were an awesome club. Hodges hit forty home runs that year, Robinson batted .338, Reese and Cox were superb on the left side of the infield. Campanella batted .325 and was the league's MVP. Snider, flawless in center field, hit twenty-nine home runs. Furillo was the best right fielder in the league and hit .295. If this wasn't enough, on June 15 the Dodgers acquired Andy Pafko from the Cubs in an eight-player swap. With Pafko in left field, that always troublesome position was now filled with one of the league's best.

Roe posted an incredible 22–3 record, Newcombe won twenty, Erskine sixteen, Clyde King fourteen, Branca thirteen. The Dodgers led the league in runs, hits, doubles, home runs, runs batted in, stolen bases, batting average, slugging average, double plays. Beginning with the second week of May, they were in first place every single day of the regular season. On August 11 they were thirteen and a half games ahead of the second-place Giants.

On August 12 the Giants began the most remarkable stretch run in baseball history. Led by three strong right-handers, Sal (The Barber) Maglie, Larry Jansen, and Jim Hearn, Durocher's team ran off a sixteen-game winning streak and kept going, winning thirty-seven of their last forty-four games.

Although they could not compare to the Dodgers in talent, the Giants had a fine, solid club, including Monte Irvin, Alvin Dark, Eddie Stanky, Henry Thompson, Bobby Thomson, Wes Westrum, Whitey Lockman, Don Mueller, and an infectious ball-playing genius in center field, an awesome rookie named Willie Mays, the most gifted youngster to come into the league since Pete Reiser.

Many people believe the Dodgers collapsed that September. Not so. True, they slipped to a 14–13 record, but each game they lost was lost forever, because of the Giants' remorseless forward motion. It was virtually impossible to gain an inch of ground.

The two clubs came into the last day of the season in a flat-footed tie. The Giants were playing the Braves in Boston, the Dodgers the Phillies in Philadelphia. The Giant game ended first, Jansen beating Boston by a 3–2 score. The Dodger game seemed to go on forever. Indeed, it went fourteen innings, as for the third year in a row the Dodgers and Phillies battled into extra innings to decide the National League pennant.

Down 8–5, the Dodgers had rallied for three in the eighth to tie the score. Don Newcombe, who had pitched a shutout the night before, came to the mound. Newk pitched gutty one-hit shutout ball for the next five and two-thirds until, dog-tired, he was relieved by Brooklyn's seventh pitcher, Bud Podbielan. Working in relief for the Phillies, and firing shutout ball for six innings, was their ace, Robin Roberts.

Robinson had saved the game for the Dodgers in the last of the twelfth with a miraculous two-out catch of Eddie Waitkus' liner with the bases loaded. Now Jackie came up with two out in the top of the fourteenth and lined a Roberts fastball into the left-field stands for the most dramatic home run in Brooklyn history. Podbielan held the Phillies in the last half of the inning, and the Dodgers headed into a playoff with the Giants.

The Giants won the flip of the coin and elected to play the first game in Ebbets Field, finishing the series in the Polo Grounds.

The playoff is stark history. The Giants won the first game behind Hearn, 3–1. The winning blow was a two-run home run by Bobby Thomson against Branca. Thomson no doubt figured that was the biggest home run he would ever hit.

The next day the brilliant rookie Clem Labine shut out the Giants in the Polo Grounds, 10–0.

In a season filled with "big" games, "crucial" games, this last one was no longer big, no longer crucial. It was, simply, everything. With the two bitter, ancient rivals opposing each other, with its air of tension, drama, and inevitability, it was a show no Hollywood dream merchant would have dared conjure up. To add to the fine edge of dramatic perfection, each club had its ace on the mound. Newcombe, pitching for the third time in five days, was opposed by Maglie, the superb curveballer, for Dodger fans the most hated of all the Giants.

The Dodgers broke open a 1–1 tie with three in the top of the eighth, and with Newcombe pitching strongly it looked like for all their magnificent heroics the Giants were going to come up short.

The last of the ninth began ominously. Al Dark singled to right. Don Mueller followed with another hit to right. The Giants' big hitter, Monte Irvin, was next. He fouled out to Hodges near the box seats. Whitey Lockman, a tough left-handed batter, sliced a double to left, scoring Dark and setting the tying run on second.

From the Dodger bullpen the word was that Erskine's curve did not look sharp, but Branca was popping the ball. The gutty Newcombe left, replaced by Branca. The batter was Bobby Thomson. The first pitch was a fastball for a strike. A rather juicy strike, and Thomson was later to wonder why he hadn't swung at it. Branca came back with the same pitch, in the same place. This time Thomson did not let it go by. He lined it into the left-field stands, above the head of a frustrated, helpless Andy Pafko.

A newspaperman quoted Jackie Robinson: "One minute we were in the World Series, the next minute we're in the clubhouse." Only, the reporter noted, Jackie didn't say "clubhouse."

Whatever house they were in, it was a depressed one for the Dodgers that winter.

To his credit, O'Malley did not fire his manager. Rather than blame his bouncy little skipper, O'Malley chose to recognize the Giants' heroics as the cause of defeat and decided to stay with Charlie, for one more year at least. It was a smart move.

Not only did the Dodgers fall off in all offensive departments in 1952, they also lost Newcombe to the Army for two years. To make things even worse, Roe dropped from twenty-two wins to eleven, Erskine from sixteen to fourteen, King from fourteen to two, Branca from thirteen to a sore-armed four. Dressen had to rebuild his pitching staff under the fire of a long season and another challenge from a supremely confident Giant club. (The Giants also had their problems. Irvin broke his ankle in spring training and was lost most of the season, Mays went into the service in May, and both Maglie and Jansen had their effectiveness curtailed by back injuries.)

The skillful Dressen pieced together his pitching staff by adding rookie Billy Loes, Ben Wade, and Joe Black, all right-handers. Loes, a moody, erratic New York City product, possessor of an excellent curveball, won thirteen and lost eight. Wade was 11–9. The key, however, was Black. The twenty-eight-year-old rookie turned in a remarkable year, remarkable for what he did and equally remarkable because he was never able

119

to do it again. Black was simply superb coming out of the bullpen. Big, strong, tough, he won fifteen, lost four, and saved another fifteen, doing it with an overpowering fastball and sharp little breaking pitch.

Dressen took his team into first place in mid-May, and they were never headed, despite a late-season scare from the Giants, who were trying to crank up another miracle. But this year Joe Black wouldn't let it happen, and the Dodgers came in four and a half ahead of Leo's Giants.

In the American League, Casey Stengel's Yankees had taken a fourth consecutive pennant. And they were about to take a fourth consecutive World Series, in spite of Duke Snider's four home runs and some fine pitching by Carl Erskine. Erskine was one of those killer athletes who don't look the part. Handsome, open-faced, with a pleasant smile, the trimly built right-hander pitched with a painful sore arm throughout most of his career. He was an extremely competitive performer who threw a sharp, tough-to-hit overhand curve.

After having been knocked out in the sixth inning of game two, Erskine came back to start game five on just two days' rest. The Series was tied at two games apiece. The Dodgers took a 4–0 lead into the bottom of the fifth. The Yankees then got to Erskine for five runs. Dressen, however, never wavered. He let his pitcher stay in, despite the battering. Charlie knew what he was doing. Erskine settled down again and retired the last nineteen men he faced, the Dodgers winning it in the eleventh, 6–5.

That was the high-water mark for the Dodgers in that Series. The Yankees took the next two games, at Ebbets Field. There was a slight flurry in the seventh game. With the bases loaded and two out in the last half of the seventh inning, and the Yankees leading 4–2, Jackie Robinson hit a high infield pop. For a moment there was some confusion among the Yankee infielders, and no one moved for the ball. At the last minute, second baseman Billy Martin came charging in and took the ball just before it dropped.

In 1953 Joe Black lost his effectiveness, won only six, and was no longer the stopper. The slack in the bullpen was picked up by new-comer Jim Hughes and Clem Labine. Labine, a right-hander with an assortment of sharp-sinking curveballs, had developed into a particularly brilliant relief pitcher, perhaps the best the Dodgers ever had.

Erskine had his greatest year in 1953, winning twenty and losing just six. Russ Meyer, acquired from the Phillies, won fifteen, and Billy Loes won fourteen. Preacher Roe, at age thirty-eight, still had enough left for an 11–3 record.

As difficult as it was to break into the Dodger lineup, room had to be made for rookie Jim Gilliam. The switch-hitting youngster took over at second base; Robinson divided his season between third base and left field. (Pafko had been traded to the Braves.)

The '53 Dodgers were another awesome aggregation. Their 208 home runs constituted the second highest total in big-league history. Demonstrating a remarkable versatility—along with their power was a .285 team average—they led the league in home runs for the fifth consecutive year and in stolen bases for the *eighth* consecutive time. Five .300 hitters were in the lineup, led by Carl Furillo's league-leading .344. Furillo was the eighth, and last, Brooklyn Dodger to win the batting title.

The Dodgers ran away from the league with a sizzling July and August record of 48–14, won an all-time Brooklyn high of 105 games, and raced home thirteen games ahead of second-place Milwaukee.

If the New York Yankees were impressed by any of this, they did not show it. Stengel's team, an irresistible force in those years, took an unprecedented fifth straight pennant and fifth straight world championship, four games to two. In game three Erskine brought deep pride to Flatbush when he fanned a record fourteen Yankees in a 3–2 win.

In game six, a dramatic home run into the right-field stands by Furillo tied the game in the ninth inning, but in the bottom of the inning a ground-ball single by Billy Martin—a record-tying twelfth series hit for Martin—drove in the winning run and made October bridesmaids of the Dodgers for the seventh time. Their 0–7 record in World Series play was now a huge embarrassment.

In spite of his October disappointment, Charlie Dressen was riding high. He had become the first manager in Dodger history to win two consecutive pennants, if not wiping out then certainly soothing the memory of 1951. So he decided to challenge O'Malley's policy of writing one-year contracts for Brooklyn managers. Charlie not only asked for a three-year pact but couched the request more or less in the terms of an ultimatum. O'Malley would not yield—nobody ever pushed the corpulent lawyer around—and Dressen found himself boxed in. Boxed in, in this context, meant out, and the Dodgers found themselves in the market for a new field boss.

After weeks of speculation, the new man was hired. The Dodgers had decided to dip into their organization and hire a company man—Walter (Smokey) Alston. Alston was such a stranger to Brooklyn fans that he was known as "Walter Who?" that winter. But he was no stranger to the Dodger players, having worked with many of them while winning minor league pennants at St. Paul and Montreal.

A man of frightening physical strength, which he was not averse in asserting to keep his players in line, Alston took over a difficult assignment. The team, it was said, was good enough to play and win without a manager. It was a club that had won handily and was expected to win again.

Signed by the Cardinals in the early thirties, Alston's big-league experience consisted of one time at bat and one strikeout, in 1936. This inglorious record did not faze Alston, however; in fact, nothing daunted this strong, quiet man who believed in his own abilities. As far as his big-league record was concerned, he knew that he had had at least one more at bat than Joe McCarthy, who had gone on to manage, among others, Hornsby, Ruth, Gehrig, DiMaggio, and Williams.

But the 1954 Dodgers did the unexpected—they came in second. It was a year of disappointments. Newcombe, back from the service, won only nine games. Erskine dropped to an 18–15 mark. Preacher Roe and Billy Cox were at the end of their careers. Campanella, playing all year with a hand injury, batted a meager .207.

Durocher got the Giants into first place in early June, and they were never headed.

Recognizing the problems he had faced, the Dodgers stayed with Alston, Walter signing another of what were to become his famous one-year contracts (there would be twenty-three of them before he retired after the 1976 season).

The 1955 club made its intentions known early. It rushed from the starting gate with a surge and wreaked unparalleled havoc upon the league. They opened with a record ten straight wins and twenty-two victories in their first twenty-four games. Campanella, recovered from his injury, batted .318 and won his third MVP award. Snider hit 42 home runs and led the league with 136 runs batted in. Erskine and Loes had winning years; so did rookie Roger Craig, who was brought up in July along with Don Bessent. Bessent and another rookie, Ed Roebuck, teamed with Labine to give the Dodgers the most formidable bullpen in their history.

But the year belonged to Don Newcombe, and the big guy went at it with flair and unalloyed joy. Not only did he win twenty and lose just five, but Newk also swung a potent bat. He hit .359 and belted seven home runs, a league record for a pitcher.

Though they slowed their winning pace somewhat late in the summer, their quick getaway enabled the Dodgers to finish a comfortable thirteen and a half games ahead of an ever-stronger Milwaukee club.

Once more October brought the Yankee specter. Stengel's team, having finally lost a pennant the year before, were back again, intent upon regaining what they believed rightfully theirs—the championship of the world.

After the first two games it looked like business as usual in a Dodger-Yankee Series. Whitey Ford beat Newcombe in the first game and Tommy Byrne beat Loes in the second, both played at Yankee Stadium. The Dodgers, however, fought back, taking the next three at Ebbets Field, thanks to some fine pitching by Johnny Podres, Clem Labine, and Roger Craig and power hitting by Hodges, Campanella, and Snider, who had another four-home-run Series.

Moving back to Yankee Stadium, up three games to two, the Dodgers were on the brink of taking it all now. In game six, however, they ran up against one of the most artful carvers of all time, lefty Whitey Ford. With the vast distances of the Stadium at his back, Ford was able to neutralize Brooklyn's right-handed power, pitching a four-hitter and winning easily, 5–1.

So they moved into a seventh game, that most pulse-quickening of sporting events. For the Yankees it was merely another opportunity to reassert their primacy in the world of baseball; for the Dodgers, however, it was one more chance to wipe out the humiliations of the past, to give a fanatical following what it had been hungering for for more than half a century.

The opposing pitchers were a pair of left-handers, Tommy Byrne, who had won the second game for the Yankees, and twenty-two-year-old Johnny Podres, winner of game three

for the Dodgers. Podres was a tough-minded, hard-throwing kid who had grown up in the Adirondacks listening to Red Barber broadcasting the Dodger games, dreaming of someday pitching for Brooklyn. Now here he was, with more than his dream's worth, entrusted with a pitcher's most precious assignment—the seventh game of the World Series.

The two lefties dueled tightly on that October 4 afternoon before over 62,000 people. In the top of the fourth Hodges singled in a run for a 1–0 Dodger lead. In the top of the sixth Hodges drove in another run with a sacrifice fly. In that inning Alston sent up George Shuba to pinch-hit for second baseman Don Zimmer. Shuba made out, but a fateful switching of players had been set in motion. In the bottom of the sixth the versatile Jim Gilliam, who had been playing left field, moved in to take over second, and a little Cuban with swift feet, quick bat, and mile-wide smile, Sandy Amoros, went to left field.

(Interestingly enough, each side had its most dynamic player on the bench with injuries in this last game, Robinson for the Dodgers and Mantle for the Yankees, although Mantle did pinch-hit, unsuccessfully, in the seventh inning.)

In the bottom of the sixth Billy Martin opened with a walk. Gil McDougald beat out a bunt inside the third-base line. The batter was Yogi Berra, one of baseball's most lethal clutch hitters. Normally a pronounced pull hitter, Berra lofted a high fly along the left-field line. With the outfield swung around, it looked like a sure extra-base hit. Gil McDougald, taking off from first, certainly thought so. Billy Martin, the runner on second with a better angle on the ball, wasn't so sure, and he held up.

Amoros was going after the ball at top speed, the big glove on his right hand stretched far out. As Sandy bore down on the fence, Johnny Podres stood on the mound like a statue, breath held, thinking, *Is he going to get it?* One of the great moments in all of World Series history is the sight of the small, winged-footed Amoros crossing the grass in Yankee Stadium's left field, bearing down on the fence, eyes skyward, glove out.

A few feet from the fence the ball dropped into that straining glove. (It is doubtful that the right-handed-throwing Gilliam, having to reach across his body, could have caught it.) Turning on the brakes, Amoros whirled, fired a strike to relay man Reese—perfectly positioned in short left—who whirled and fired another strike to Hodges at first, doubling up McDougald, who had actually turned second base, so sure was he that the ball would drop.

It was a heart-stopping moment. Taking a deep breath, Podres went back to work, retiring the side. Inning after inning he continued firing his shutout, mixing change-ups with a riding fastball. Pitch by pitch he was carving his and Amoros' names into baseball history.

With two out in the bottom of the ninth, Elston Howard (the Yankees' first black player, eight years after the arrival of Robinson) grounded to short, was thrown out by Reese, and a riptide of emotion tore through the borough of Brooklyn.

They were World Champions now, with but two years of life left (though no one knew this at the time, of course). They were also the oldest club in the league, averaging thirty-two years of age. Reese was thirty-seven, Furillo thirty-four, Campanella thirty-four, Robinson thirty-seven. A strong Milwaukee club, headed by sluggers Hank Aaron, Eddie Mathews, and Joe Adcock, and pitchers Warren Spahn and Lew Burdette, was set to take them on.

The Braves took the lead in mid-July and fought off the Dodgers and a power-laden Cincinnati club all summer. With Gilliam the team's only .300 hitter, the Dodgers battled gamely all year, powered by Snider's league-leading forty-three home runs and a sensational

year by Don Newcombe who won twenty-seven and lost but seven.

Milwaukee slipped to a 14–13 record in September, while the Dodgers cranked up to an 18–10 mark and closed the gap, helped by the superb pitching of a new and most unlikely Dodger hero: Sal Maglie. Maglie had been waived to Cleveland the year before and in May of '56 acquired by Brooklyn. Watching Maglie fire his curves on their behalf now was a joy for Brooklyn fans, and all past sins were forgiven. The thirty-nine-year-old Maglie coaxed thirteen wins out of his ancient right arm, culminating with a no-hitter against the Phillies on September 25.

On the final day of the season the Dodgers were at home against Pittsburgh, with a one-game lead. All they needed was a win to clinch their fourth pennant in five years. Snider hit an explosive three-run homer in the first inning, added another later, Amoros also hit two, and the Dodgers nailed their last Brooklyn pennant to the flagpole. The score was 8–6.

The Yankees were once again waiting in the October shadows, and the last Brooklyn World Series was to feature the most spectacular feat of pitching in World Series history. Nothing that had gone before could compare to what journeyman right-hander Don Larsen inflicted upon Brooklyn in game five on October 8, 1956.

With the Series tied at two games apiece, Larsen, who had been shelled in the second inning of game two, pitched the only perfect game in World Series history (and only the fifth in big-league history since 1900).

Working out of a no-windup delivery, the big right-hander mowed down in order the following lineup: Gilliam, Reese, Snider, Robinson, Hodges, Amoros, Furillo, Campanella, Maglie, and, for the last out, pinch hitter Dale Mitchell. Larsen worked with remarkable efficiency, throwing just ninety-seven pitches and going to a full count only on the game's second batter, Reese.

Buried under Larsen's masterpiece was a superior performance by Maglie, who pitched a five-hitter, losing 2–0.

The following day Labine produced a gem of his own, winning a 1–0, ten-inning duel against Bob Turley. Going into a seventh game once again, the Yankees turned it into a shambles, winning behind Johnny Kucks, 10–0. Over the last twenty-eight innings the Dodgers could manage but seven hits and one run.

In the 1–0 game the winning run was driven home by a scorching line drive off the bat of Robinson. It turned out to be Jackie's last base hit as a Dodger. In December he was sold to the Giants for $35,000. Jackie, however, had already planned to retire. Approaching his thirty-eighth birthday, his once-blazing talents had cooled. The dazzling speed was gone, the hair-trigger reflexes dulled.

The proud, combative Robinson never returned to baseball. He went into executive positions with various corporations, became a confidant of New York Governor Nelson Rockefeller, and remained, as ever, an outspoken foe of bigotry and discrimination. Illness clouded his last years, draining the vigor from that once-powerful physique. White-haired, diabetic, his eyesight failing, Robinson died on October 24, 1972, at the age of fifty-three. It is given to few men to leave behind a strong and positive legacy. Jackie Robinson is one of the few. His electrifying athletic abilities and his tenaciously proud and indomitable spirit helped bring baseball out of the decay of intolerance and discrimination into a new and enduring era of equality.

There were some promising faces on the '57 Dodgers, among them twenty-year-old sophomore pitcher Don Drysdale who won seventeen. Young bonus baby Sandy Koufax, in his third year of part-time play, was still having trouble finding home plate, though his 122 strikeouts in 104 innings indicated something was alive in his left arm.

Newcombe dropped from the heights to an 11–12 year. Podres, back from a year's stint in the Navy, won twelve. Maglie had shot his bolt the year before and won only six before being waived to the Yankees. Erskine had a sore arm much of the year, winning only five.

Reese, now thirty-eight, played half the season at third base, yielding his shortstop position to Charley Neal. Campanella no longer swung with his old authority. Furillo, Hodges, and Snider hit well, Duke poling forty home runs for the fifth year in a row. But it wasn't enough.

Never higher than second place all year, the Dodgers dropped into third at the end of July and stayed there for the rest of the way, finishing eleven games behind the Milwaukee Braves, who were led by Henry Aaron, now in full bloom.

By 1957 Charles Ebbets' majestic baseball palace had become obsolete. Its seating capacity was too small; its parking facilities were woefully inadequate. In addition, the general area around the ball park was deteriorating rapidly.

The summer of '57 was filled with a welter of conflicting stories. At times O'Malley seemed to be searching for a site to build a new ball park, and at other times he seemed to be allowing himself to be wooed by the city of Los Angeles.

Exactly when the idea of a franchise shift first came to O'Malley is not known. The Boston Braves' move to Milwaukee in 1953 had been highly successful, pumping new life into a moribund franchise. Even with championship teams, the Dodgers had been barely breaking the million mark in attendance. They were making money all right; it was just that O'Malley thought they should be making more.

While talk was going on in New York about a new stadium for the Dodgers, O'Malley had already bought from the Cubs their Los Angeles franchise in the Pacific Coast League. Perhaps it was the orientation of their own minds, but

New York's politicians thought O'Malley was bluffing about the possibility of absconding to Los Angeles. O'Malley, as sharp and as devious as any politico, surely was capable of stage-managing such a charade. Finally it did become a charade, but not the one Brooklyn fans were hoping for. While asserting all summer long that there was still a chance for the Dodgers to remain, O'Malley was committing himself to Los Angeles and at the same time talking Giants' owner Horace Stoneham into moving his club to San Francisco. Thus, baseball's greatest rivalry would be transplanted to the West Coast. The forthright Stoneham announced as early as mid-July that he would recommend to his board of directors the club be moved "elsewhere." On August 19 a board vote made the Giants' move official.

O'Malley continued to keep his plans to himself, although by now all signs were pointing to California. Pitting one major city against the other, O'Malley played his game shrewdly. On September 16 the city of Los Angeles agreed, subject to council approval, to transfer over 300 acres of an area called Chavez Ravine to O'Malley for $4,400,000. The county would then spend several million dollars to grade the site (which was a few minutes' drive from downtown L.A.) and several million more to build connecting roads and freeways. The city also agreed to pay O'Malley $2,500,000 for the small, outmoded Wrigley Field ball park in Los Angeles. On October 7 the city council voted its approval of the deal, and the next day O'Malley accepted.

It was done.

In 1934 Bill Terry had facetiously asked the question: "Is Brooklyn still in the league?" Twenty-three years later he had his answer.

It is September 1946, and a packed house has risen for the playing of the National Anthem at Ebbets Field.

Dick Whitman, a swift-footed outfielder who played for the Dodgers from 1946–49, is shown here being tagged out at home while trying to stretch a triple into an inside-the-park home run. The catcher is Bill Salkeld of Pittsburgh. The date was May 27, 1946. The Dodgers won a doubleheader from the Pirates that day by identical 4–3 scores.

Jackie Robinson with Montreal in 1946.

Durocher and Rickey during spring training, 1947, just before Chandler lowered the boom on Leo.

History is about to be made. It is April 11, 1947. The Dodgers and Yankees are about to take the field for an exhibition game at Ebbets Field. Playing with the Dodgers for the first time is Jackie Robinson, newly promoted from Montreal. Left to right, first basemen Ed Stevens and Howie Schultz, acting manager Clyde Sukeforth, Robinson, and coaches Jake Pitler and Ray Blades.

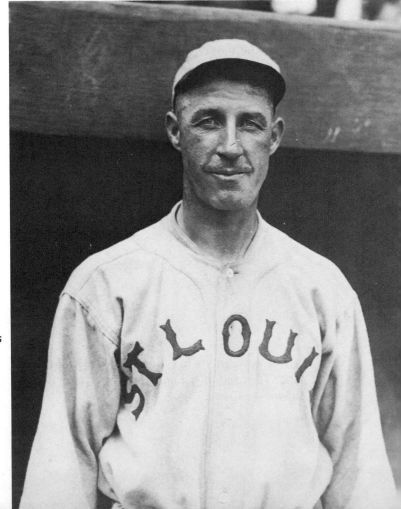

Burt Shotton, shown here with the Cardinals in 1919.

Eddie Stanky in 1947. The scrappy, aggressive, baseball-wise Stanky was obtained from the Cubs in 1944 and stayed with the Dodgers through the 1947 season, when he was traded to Boston in order to open up second base for Robinson. A patient man at the plate, Eddie waited out 148 walks in 1947 and 137 the next year, both league-leading totals. The 148 is still a National League record (tied by Jim Wynn of Houston in 1969). His most memorable hit as a Dodger came on June 22, 1947, in Cincinnati, when he singled with one out in the ninth inning to break up Ewell Blackwell's bid for a second consecutive no-hitter.

John (Spider) Jorgensen. Spider hit .274 in his rookie year in 1947, but the arrival of Billy Cox the next year put him on the bench, where he remained until dealt to the Giants in 1950.

Bobby Bragan was a utility man for the Dodgers from 1943–48, with two years out for military service. Later, he became a colorful and innovative manager for the Pirates, Indians, and Braves.

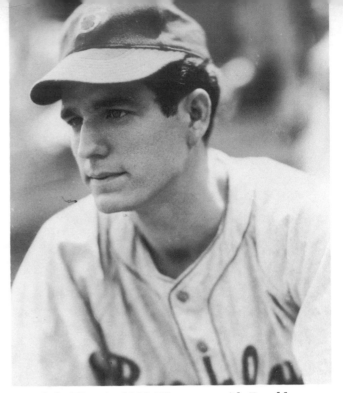

Clyde King in 1947. King was with Brooklyn for parts of six seasons between 1944 and 1952. His best year was 1951 when he was 14–7, most of it in relief.

Jackie Robinson in 1947.

Stan Rojek in 1946. Stan was another fine young shortstop developed by the Dodgers who was unemployable in Brooklyn because of Reese. He was traded to Pittsburgh in 1948.

Joe Hatten joined the Dodger pitching staff in 1946 and remained until traded to Chicago in June 1951. Joe's best year was 1947, when he was 17–8.

Members of the Brooklyn Sym-phony, which made Ebbets Field a more colorful—and louder—place in which to watch a ball game. The two players being entertained are Spider Jorgensen on the left and Bobby Bragan.

Carl Furillo in 1947.

Hank Behrman in 1947. The easygoing
Behrman was a willing worker and a hard
thrower. Starting and relieving, he was 11–5
in his rookie year of 1946. In 1949 he was
traded to the Giants.

By the middle of the 1947 season only five
men remained from the '41 pennant
winners. In the rear are Hugh Casey (left)
and Pee Wee Reese; in the front, left to right,
Pete Reiser, Cookie Lavagetto, and Dixie
Walker. By the time the 1949 season opened,
only Reese remained.

Dan Bankhead joined the Dodgers in mid-
season in 1947, and the right-hander became
the first black to pitch in the big leagues.
Dan was roughed up in his few appearances
and did not return until 1950, his only full
season, when he was 9–4. He pitched a few
times in 1951, did not fare well, and faded
from the big-league scene.

Gene Hermanski joined the Dodgers in 1943, went into the service for two years, and rejoined the team in 1946, remaining until traded to the Cubs in June 1951. An outfielder with good power, Gene's best years were 1948–50, when he hit .290, .299, .298.

In 1946 young Ralph Branca was all smiles, and the future was bright. In 1947 he was the ace, with twenty-one wins. There were several more productive years, and then . . .

In 1946 the Dodgers brought up a fine young catcher named Bruce Edwards. He hit .267 in his rookie year and caught well. In 1947 he was the regular catcher as the Dodgers won the pennant, batting .295. He was only twenty-four and seemed set for many years. In 1948 another catcher joined the Dodgers. His name was Roy Campanella. The Dodgers had still another catcher, named Gil Hodges, but they made a first baseman out of him. Catching less and less each year, Edwards was finally traded to the Cubs in 1951.

Harry Taylor in 1947. This fine right-hander
was moving right along with a 10–5 record
in 1947 when he hurt his arm. The snap in
his curveball never came back. He was 2–7
the next year and then left Brooklyn. He tried
a comeback with the Red Sox a few years
later, but it didn't pan out.

Eddie Miksis joined the Dodgers at the age
of seventeen in the war year of 1944. After
coming out of the service in 1946, he
remained with the team as a utility man until
traded with Hatten, Hermanski, and
Edwards to the Cubs in June 1951 in the
Andy Pafko deal.

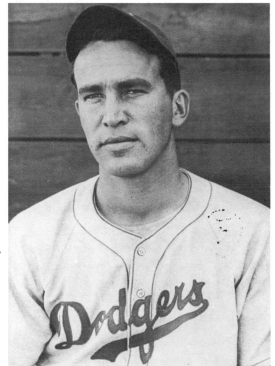

Hard-throwing right-hander Hal Gregg was
one of those youngsters caught in Branch
Rickey's wartime net. Gregg was Brooklyn's
ace in 1945, winning eighteen and losing
thirteen. His win totals dwindled thereafter,
and he was traded to Pittsburgh after the
'47 season.

Al Gionfriddo. He was with Brooklyn for only part of the season in 1947 and batted a humble .177. But that October Joe DiMaggio would make him a hero.

Here we have two very determined men: Cardinal catcher Del Rice, who has the plate nicely blocked; and Gene Hermanski, who is getting in through the back door. Spider Jorgensen and Umpire Bill Stewart are interested spectators. This occurred at Ebbets Field on May 6, 1947.

Winning pitcher Hugh Casey and Cookie Lavagetto in the Dodger clubhouse moments after Cookie's dramatic blow.

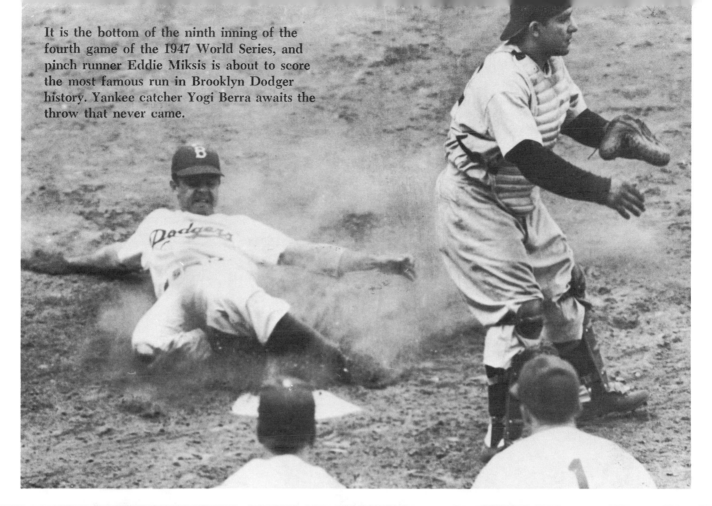

It is the bottom of the ninth inning of the fourth game of the 1947 World Series, and pinch runner Eddie Miksis is about to score the most famous run in Brooklyn Dodger history. Yankee catcher Yogi Berra awaits the throw that never came.

Al Gionfriddo has just stepped into the history books with his spectacular grab of DiMaggio's bid for a three-run, game-tying home run in the sixth inning of the sixth game of the 1947 World Series. Another handsome relief stint by Casey saved this game for Brooklyn.

Left to right, Eddie Stanky, Pee Wee Reese, and a returned-from-exile Leo Durocher in spring training at Trujillo City, Dominican Republic. The date is March 4, 1948. Two days later Stanky was traded to the Braves, opening up second base for Robinson.

138

Billy Cox in 1948.

Preacher Roe.

Back at Ebbets Field again, Durocher greets Burt Shotton who has become, for the moment, just another fan holding his scorecard.

In action: The greatest double-play combination in Brooklyn Dodger history.

140

Jackie Robinson about to slide in safely with a steal of home. It's August 22, 1948, at Ebbets Field. The catcher is Bill Salkeld, the batter Billy Cox, the umpire Jocko Conlon.

Gil Hodges in 1948.

Roy Campanella when he was catching for the Baltimore Elite Giants in the Negro League.

Duke Snider in 1948.

Few pitchers, if any, ever threw the ball harder than Rex Barney. He was another of the youngsters Rickey signed during the war. The eighteen-year-old Barney was 2–2 in 1943, then entered military service for two years. When he returned in 1946 his future seemed limitless. "As soon as he gets his control," everyone said. Now and then he had his control, and when he did he was almost unhittable. On September 9, 1948, he was quite unhittable at the Polo Grounds, stopping the Giants without a hit. He was 15–13 that year, his brilliance flashing on and off like a neon light. He was 9–8 the next year, the brilliance showing itself less frequently now. The next year was his last. He pitched but thirty-four innings, walking forty-eight men. He had become, quite frankly, a menace out on the mound. He left the big leagues at the age of twenty-six.

The 1949 All-Star Game was played at Ebbets Field on July 12, with black players participating for the first time. Left to right, Roy Campanella, Larry Doby of the Indians, Don Newcombe, Jackie Robinson.

Duke Snider has just hit a jackpot home run. The welcoming committee is, left to right, Reese, Campanella, Hodges.

Don Newcombe in 1949.

This lovely piece of baseball choreography took place at Ebbets Field on August 23, 1949. Carl Furillo has just made a shoestring catch on a ball hit by Chuck Diering of the Cardinals (note the ball in the webbing of his glove). Also converging on the ball were center fielders Duke Snider (top) and second baseman Jackie Robinson. The umpire kicking up his heels and making the out call is Jocko Conlon.

The rites of October are being performed by two joyous young Dodgers at Yankee Stadium before the start of the 1949 World Series. Campanella, left, and Newcombe.

Jack Banta, whose brilliant relief pitching on the last day of the 1949 season gave Brooklyn a pennant. The twenty-four-year-old Banta was 10–6 that year, and what looked like a brilliant career lay ahead. The next year, however, he came down with an arm injury and was through.

Preacher Roe being interviewed after shutting out the Yankees 1–0 in game two of the 1949 World Series.

National League President Ford Frick presenting Jackie Robinson with a gold plaque in recognition of Jackie's having been voted the National League's Most Valuable Player in 1949. The ceremony took place at Ebbets Field on the night of July 6, 1950.

Ervin Martin Pavliecivich did everyone a favor by changing his name to Erv Palica. With the Dodgers from 1947–54, Palica had a world of stuff but turned out to be another one of those brilliant youngsters destined to leave his promise unfulfilled. The right-hander's best year was 1950, when he was 13–8. Two years of military service and a sore arm followed.

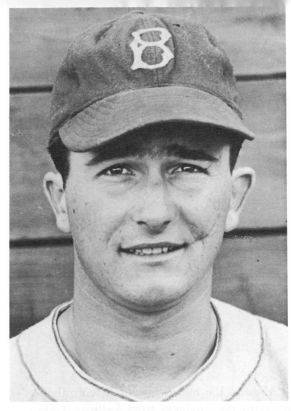

Thunder over Brooklyn. Left to right, Snider, Hodges, Robinson, Reese, Campanella.

Cal Abrams, the man who didn't score that day. With the Dodgers from 1949–52, Cal's best year was 1951, when he hit .280.

Jackie Robinson and Branch Rickey.

Dick Sisler—running down to first base—has just lined into the left-field stands the home run that gave the Phillies the pennant. A disheartened Don Newcombe stands all alone on the mound. It's October 2, 1950, and all those people at Ebbets Field were suddenly very quiet.

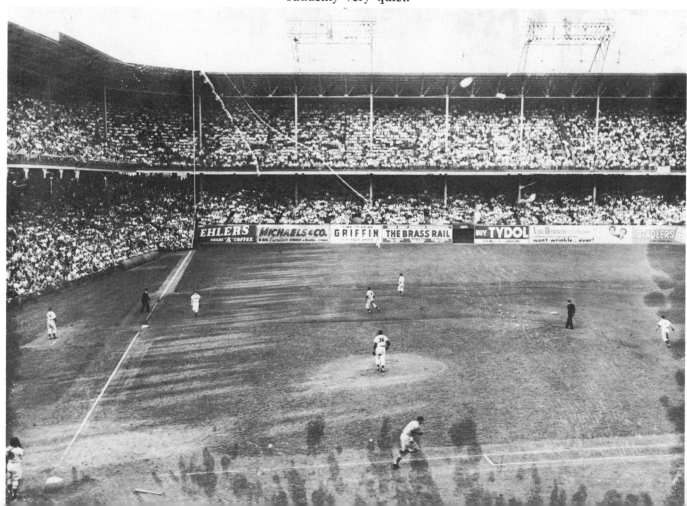

It's April 1951, and Gil Hodges is churning up a cloud of Ebbets Field real estate as he scores a split second before Phillies catcher Andy Seminick receives the relay.

Dodger skipper Chuck Dressen in 1951.

Cincinnati third baseman Chuck Dressen in 1926.

Dick Williams was a utility outfielder with Brooklyn from 1951–56, seeing limited service. He later went on to an outstanding career as a big-league manager, winning pennants in Oakland and Boston.

Rube Walker was Brooklyn's backup catcher from 1951–57. A fine defensive catcher, Rube's best year at bat was 1952, when he hit .259.

Left to right, Carl Furillo, Duke Snider, Andy Pafko in the Dodger dugout at Wrigley Field, Chicago. It's June 15, 1951. The day before, Andy was wearing a Cub uniform. It was an eight-player swap, the Dodgers sending Hermanski, Edwards, Miksis, and Hatten to the Cubs for Pafko, catcher Rube Walker, pitcher Johnny Schmitz, and infielder Wayne Terwilliger.

Gil Hodges in 1951. Those muscles are real.

Roy Campanella, the National League's Most Valuable Player in 1951, 1953, 1955.

Campanella has just applied the tag to a sliding Willie Mays at Ebbets Field on September 2, 1951. The umpire is Al Barlick.

A moment of time in suspension. The score, according to the scoreboard, is 4–1 in favor of Brooklyn; the count on Bobby Thomson is one strike. But the confetti has begun to fall as Thomson's drive has just passed over the head of Andy Pafko into the left-field stands.

154

Thomson is now coming around third base, awaited by a jubilant reception committee. A forlorn Branca is walking away. Jackie Robinson is in the foreground.

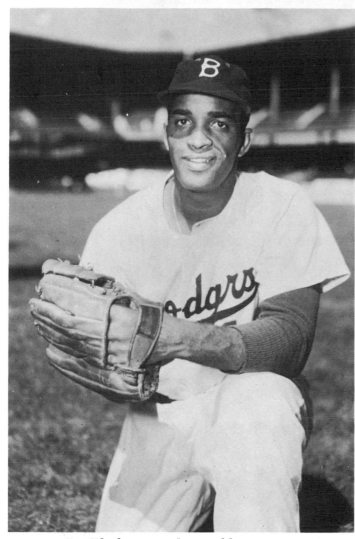

Joe Black: one unforgettable year.

Rocky Bridges was a utility man for the Dodgers in 1951–52. This engaging character was the inventor of the "hernia hit"—little loopers that the infielders strained themselves trying to get.

Bobby Morgan in 1952. On most teams Bobby would have been more than a backup third baseman. But in Brooklyn the man he was backing up was Billy Cox.

What might have been. It is a new season now. April 19, 1952, at Ebbets Field. Ralph Branca is facing Bobby Thomson for the first time since *that* time. Ralph struck him out. Truth was, Ralph Branca struck out a lot of men. He had a hopping fastball and a very sharp curve. But he never came back to form after 1951. The next year he was 4–2, shelved much of the time with a sore arm. In 1953 he was dealt to Detroit, and what should have been another splendid Brooklyn mound career never happened.

Manager Dressen (center) with some of the stalwarts of the 1952 pennant drive. Rear, left to right, Joe Black and Pee Wee Reese. Front, left to right, Duke Snider and Jackie Robinson.

Right-hander Billy Loes pitched for Brooklyn from 1950–56, when he was dealt to Baltimore. Billy had the best assortment of breaking pitches on the staff. He was a winner. For the four full years he pitched for the Dodgers his record was 50–25. He was also something of a character. He once claimed to have lost a ground ball in the sun. And to the bemusement of everyone, he picked the Yankees to win the '53 Series in six. (He was right.)

158

Ben Wade in 1952. This big right-hander pitched for Brooklyn in 1952–54. He was 11–9 in '52.

Andy Pafko was a popular player wherever he went. He was with Brooklyn in 1951–52, hitting .287 the latter year. He had a solid seventeen-year career in the National League, most of it spent with the Cubs and the Braves.

George (Shotgun) Shuba. Shuba was with the Dodgers from 1948–55, with the exception of 1951, the year they could have used his sharp pinch-hitting bat coming off the bench down the stretch. Always a utility man and pinch hitter, George's best year was 1952, when he batted .305. In 1955 his pinch-hitting average was .379.

159

Carl Erskine in action.

The second inning of the fifth game of the '52 Series. Andy Pafko has just taken a home run away from the Yankees' Gene Woodling.

Brooklyn's starting lineup for the first game of the 1952 World Series. Left to right, Cox, Reese, Snider, Robinson, Campanella, Pafko, Hodges, Furillo, Black. (Note those seventh and eighth hitters.) Black, the relief specialist, had started only twice all year. In the Series Dressen started him three times in seven days. Joe pitched well but ended up with a 1–2 record.

Carl Erskine.

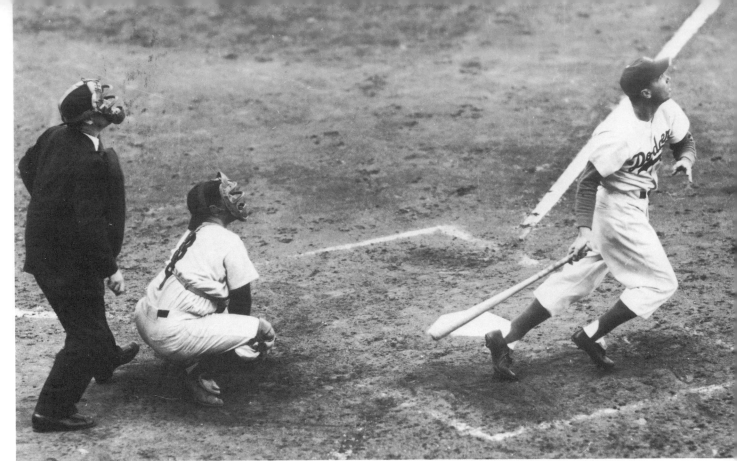

Duke Snider hit four home runs in the '52
Series. Here he is popping one of them.

The airborne gentleman is George Shuba.
It's the second inning of game five of the '52
Series. Brooklyn had the bases loaded with
one out, when Erskine tried a squeeze play.
George might as well have stayed up there
since Yogi Berra already has the ball, and
Umpire Babe Pinelli knows it.

This picture proves once and for all that umpires are human. Art Passarella called Yankee Johnny Sain out on this play, which occurred in the tenth inning of game five of the '52 Series. The ump was probably impressed with Gil Hodges' heroic stretch. Coach Bill Dickey (33) put in his two cents' worth after this dubious call, but all he got for his trouble was two pennies' change.

Game six of the '52 Series. A tense Billy Cox watches Roy Campanella gather in Gil McDougald's pop foul in the third inning.

163

Jim Hughes, who gave the Dodgers some
excellent relief pitching from 1952–56. Jim
was a tough customer with a live fastball.
In 1954 he won eight and saved twenty-four.

Billy Martin makes a desperate last-minute
running grab of Jackie Robinson's pop-up in
the seventh inning of the seventh game of
the '52 Series. There were two out and the
bases loaded at the time. A running Robinson
and an anxious Phil Rizzuto are watching.

Johnny Podres in 1953, just twenty years old.
He was 9–4 that year, 11–7 the next, and
had the big one coming up.

Clem Labine, probably the greatest relief pitcher the Dodgers ever had. He threw a sinker that was guaranteed to give his infielders steady work. Clem pitched for Brooklyn from 1950 until they left town. His best year was 1955, when he was 13–5. Though remembered as a premier reliever, Labine's two shining moments in Brooklyn came as a starter—his 10–0 shutout of the Giants in the second game of the '51 playoff, and a 1–0 ten-inning blanking of the Yankees in game six of the '56 Series.

In twelve years of major-league play Preacher Roe batted .110. He hit three doubles and one home run. The home run came on July 7, 1953, at Pittsburgh. Roe's teammates were not unmindful of the historic moment and laid out a carpet of towels for the slugger when he returned to the dugout.

It is Sunday afternoon, September 6, 1953, at the Polo Grounds, and the Brooklyn Dodgers and New York Giants have gathered together. The occasion was a meeting between Carl Furillo and Leo Durocher in front of the Giant dugout. A few moments before, Furillo had been hit by a pitch thrown by the Giants' Ruben Gomez. Furillo thought unkindly of this and when he got to first base began an exchange of unpleasantries with the Giant manager. Furillo told Leo to come out and say that. Leo beckoned Carl forward. Carl charged. Somewhere at the bottom of the group lie Furillo and Durocher. The brawl was limited to those two; the other gentlemen are either observers or peacemakers.

Russ Meyer. The Dodgers acquired this colorful right-hander from the Phillies. He pitched for Brooklyn from 1953–55. He did his best work in '53 with a 15–5 record.

A day later, and Carl Furillo is all smiles once again as he shows off his brand-new plaster cast to Dressen and Reese. Carl's finger had been broken the day before—not, as he would have preferred, on the head of Leo Durocher but stepped upon by a peacemaker. Furillo sat out the rest of the season, freezing his .344 batting average and giving him the batting crown by two points over the Cardinals' Red Schoendienst.

Furillo had recovered by World Series time, and here he is scoring in the fourth inning of the second game at Yankee Stadium, just eluding Yogi Berra's diving tag. Bill Stewart is the umpire.

This is Billy Martin doing the dipsy-do as the last out of game four of the '53 Series. Billy had tried to score on Mickey Mantle's single. Campanella obviously gave him an emphatic tag. The umpire is Art Gore. Two unhappy Yankees are watching it happen: Gene Woodling (No. 14) and Joe Collins.

Another routine play for the agile Billy Cox.
It's game five of the '53 Series, the bases are
loaded with two out in the sixth inning, and
the Yankees' Hank Bauer has just hit this
scorcher. Cox backhanded it and got the
force at third. Phil Rizzuto is the base runner
and Art Gore the umpire.

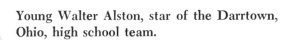

Young Walter Alston, star of the Darrtown,
Ohio, high school team.

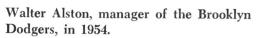

Walter Alston, manager of the Brooklyn
Dodgers, in 1954.

Spring training at Vero Beach, Florida, 1954. Four seasoned members of the Dodgers are showing off their lumber. Left to right, Hodges, Campanella, Snider, Furillo.

Rookie shortstop Don Zimmer in 1954. But Reese was still there, and all rookie shortstops were doomed to ride the bench or be traded. Zimmer rode the bench.

Wayne Belardi was with the Dodgers from 1950–54. The young left-handed-hitting Belardi had power and showed some potential. But he was a first baseman, and so was Gil Hodges.

It's December 22, 1954, and the Dodgers have just given nineteen-year-old Sandy Koufax a Christmas present—a $20,000 bonus for signing a contract. They didn't know it at the time, but they had also given themselves quite a present, though the dividends would not be paid until years later in Los Angeles. On Sandy's right is Al Campanis, then a Dodger scout; on his left, Dodgers' vice-president Fresco Thompson. The scene is the Dodger office at 215 Montague Street, Brooklyn, U.S.A.

Ed Roebuck joined the Dodgers in 1955 and contributed some very fine relief pitching over the next few years. His best year in Brooklyn was 1957, when he was 8–2.

Don Bessent joined the Dodgers in mid-season, 1955. Working primarily out of the bullpen, the hard-throwing right-hander finished up with an 8–1 record. He had another fine year in 1956, but soon after that a bad back hampered him, bringing his career to a halt.

A weary Roger Craig is being congratulated by Walter Alston after the pitcher's successful big-league debut on July 17, 1955. Craig pitched a three-hit, 6–2 victory over Cincinnati at Ebbets Field. Craig topped off a 5–3 rookie season with a win over the Yankees in the fifth game of the World Series. Note the size of Craig's hand.

A squeeze play that didn't work. Campanella tried to come in on Robinson's bunt in this game against the Cardinals on August 29, 1955. Catcher Bill Sarni is doing the honors for the Cards.

Don Hoak joined the Dodgers in 1954 and was with the team for two seasons, filling in at third base. Hoak's tough, aggressive style of play was very popular with the fans.

Johnny Podres at work.

The Amoros catch.

Johnny Podres is embraced by Gil Hodges, left, and Carl Furillo moments after pitching the Brooklyn Dodgers to their first, and only, World Championship.

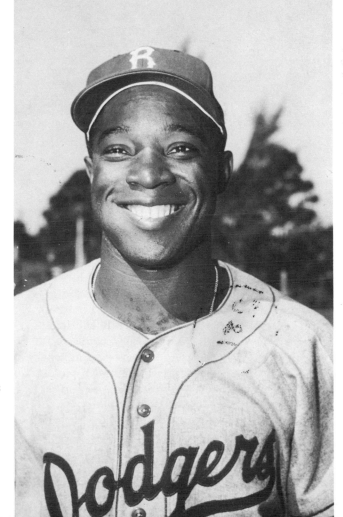

Edmundo Isasi Amoros, better known as Sandy.

The bulwarks of the Brooklyn bullpen in a group picture taken at Vero Beach in February 1956. Left to right, Ed Roebuck, Don Bessent, Clem Labine.

In 1956 the Dodgers acquired the Cubs' talented third baseman Randy Jackson as a replacement for an aging Jackie Robinson. Jackson, shown above at Vero Beach in February, was handed the job in the beginning of the season. Robinson, however, rose to the one last challenge and by mid-season was back at third base, helping the Dodgers drive to their last pennant. Jackson played well for Brooklyn, hitting .274. A knee injury took him out of most of the next season.

No pitcher ever made a more emphatic major-league debut than Karl Spooner did for the Dodgers. Brought up at the end of the 1954 season, the flamethrowing left-hander made two starts, pitched two shutouts, and in his eighteen innings of work struck out twenty-seven batters. The following season, pitching with intermittent arm trouble, he was 8–6, with flashes of brilliance. The sore arm worsened, and he never pitched again after the '55 season. Along with Rex Barney, Spooner remains one of the most intriguing "might-have-been" talents in Dodger history.

Gil Hodges in 1956.

Sal Maglie in 1956.

Jim (Junior) Gilliam showed up at Ebbets Field in 1953 and was too good to be kept out of the lineup. He became the regular second baseman. Rookie of the Year in '53, Gilliam's best season was 1956, when he batted .300.

Campy is being greeted by Carl Furillo (No. 6) and Gil Hodges after hitting a three-run homer in the bottom of the first inning against Milwaukee. The date is May 5, 1957.

It's January 1957, and Jackie Robinson has just announced his retirement.

Gino Cimoli was Brooklyn's left fielder in 1957, batting .293. Gino was a first-rate defensive outfielder.

The scoreboard tells it all as Don Larsen delivers the last pitch of his perfect game. Second baseman Billy Martin is in the background.

Charley Neal could play second, short, and third. He joined the Dodgers in 1956, hitting .287 as a part-time player. A regular the next year, he batted .270.

Duke Snider in 1956, a seasoned veteran now.

Don Drysdale, a nineteen-year-old rookie in 1956. The hard-throwing right-hander was 5–5 his first year, then gave a demonstration of future greatness with a 17–9 sophomore season.

Rookie catcher Johnny Roseboro in 1957. He saw little action that year, but after Roy Campanella's tragic accident and the move to L.A., Roseboro was the regular catcher for the next ten years.

One of the last Ebbets Field brawls occurred on June 13, 1957. Don Drysdale plunked the Braves' Johnny Logan with a pitch. Logan took exception. Words were exchanged, and then everybody spilled out on the field. Drysdale is being restrained here by another Big Don—Newcombe.

"Go West, young man."

A night game at Ebbets Field between the Dodgers and Braves on August 22, 1957. Don't think Walter O'Malley didn't notice all of those empty seats.